Soul Mates
Journey
To
Heaven

ROMANTICALLY AND MIRACULOUSLY WITH BLESSED
PASSION THERE IS NOTHING MORE INTRIGUING
OR MESMERIZING THAT SENSUALLY ENTICES THE
SOUL, OTHER THAN AN ANOINTED LOVE SERIES

THOMAS 'N DIANNIE

BALBOA.PRESS
A DIVISION OF HAY HOUSE

Balboa Press books may be ordered through booksellers or by contacting:

Balboa Press
A Division of Hay House
1663 Liberty Drive
Bloomington, IN 47403
www.balboapress.com
844-682-1282

Print information available on the last page.

ISBN: 978-1-9822-6912-8 (sc)
ISBN: 978-1-9822-6914-2 (e)

Balboa Press rev. date: 05/18/2021

CONTENTS

EPIGRAM

A friend of Thomas's said that he had to leave his wife because she was not happy. And Thomas said, "really! how did she take that?" The friend then said, "you know you live with somebody for 20 years, and you think you know them. I had no idea my wife could sing and do cartwheels at the same time".

DEDICATION

Guardian Angel, Life is vibrating with love, a guide through the unseen world where angels go freely. Any time we think of you, the one thing that we do is thank the Lord, and then we say a little prayer for you. We ask God to watch over you and shine your light before our way, even though we are apart, but most of all, we thank God for your kind and caring heart.

An Angel, unaware, touched those who a Guardian Angel loved. A divine creation through the grace of God. Brought God's love into this world for a short time. With loving-kindness, a beam of light that a Guardian Angel brought into lives.

We came together to laugh, to love, to work, and to play. Accepted God's grace that brought us together this way. We found that piece at the close of each day. Our parting has not left a void for a reason, and we remember the joy.

A friendship shared, laughing, Oh yes, these things we do miss. However, with a time we have spent together through God's holy grace and all the things we have in common that will bring us together again one day.

My life's been full and savored a dream of this love of my friend, and the good times one day will never draw to an end.

A tear, a touch, our hearts that felt so much. Perhaps our time together seemed so brief, and we lift our spirits and peace for one another, through showing your love has brought so many together.

I said a prayer for you today and know God must have heard; I felt the answer in my heart, although God spoke no word. We asked for happiness in all things great and small, but it was for God's loving care that we prayed for most of all.

John 15: 13. *Greater love hath no man than this that a man lay down his life for his friends.* The love this Guardian Angel brought together cannot be measured or understood. God's love is beyond our comprehension or imagination. The miracle, God's love is overwhelmingly present. Nothing happens perchance, everything happens for a God-given reason.

Guardian Angel, it was time to go home, and God took him by the hand, so many others could be saved through this Guardian Angel's precious memories and love.

The lives touched by this Guardian Angel can only be measured through God's love. And before we were born, God brought this precious Guardian angel into our lives unaware.

The Lord said, Guardian Angel, take me by the hand I come to take you home. The love you have shown with loving-kindness, peace, happiness, joy and laughter, far surpasses the love others have shown.

You're free, you know, get some rest and let it go, and do not think of me, I will follow the path that God had laid for me, when I had taken God's hand and heard God's call, I was free at last.

INTRODUCTION

Life is vibrating with romance and love, a guide through the unseen world where angels go freely.

Romance, soulmates from heaven, miracles of biblical proportion, suspense beyond understanding. Giving, loving, helping, joy, peace, serenity, and peace of the Holy Spirit working through Thomas and DiAnnie. This book begs to be read repeatedly, and one will get more out of it every time it's read. The Bible of life that anyone and everyone who experiences trials and tribulations can most certainly learn and relate.

Near death experiences have brought Thomas to a new understanding and appreciation for life. Helping others unconditionally and giving love through the word of God.

1 John 2:15. *Love not the world, neither the things that are in the world*. If any man loves the world, the love of the Father is not in him.

An angel dropped from heaven, also able to witness, listen, and write a supernatural miracle. Thomas has ever experienced the most incredible miracle, writing a short love paragraph of what Thomas expected of God. Through faith, prayer, and love for God. He was praying to bring Thomas a perfect, equally yoked spiritual soulmate.

As Thomas was praying, A young beautiful, radiant lady tapped Thomas on the shoulder. As Thomas turned around, and there she was, Thomases soulmate from Heaven, DiAnnie is her name. There is perfect love. Through patience and prayer, God knew the answer before Thomas.

DiAnnie's mother, Anna, was praying as well; three different souls, thousands of miles apart, could come together spiritually through prayer. Have you ever met a guardian angel?

Thomas and DiAnnie danced with the devil throughout life, and Miracles happen. The daughter, DiAnnie, an orphan, and her mother, Anna, a widow. Both of these ladies are miracles of biblical proportion, one more so than the other.

1 James: 27. *Pure religion and undefiled before God and the Father is this*. To visit the fatherless and widows in their affliction and to keep himself unspotted from the world.

The loving Spirit that is Holy, moving throughout the earth with an abundance of precious life, a gift Jesus Christ our Lord left us before ascending into heaven.

DiAnnie's, a sweet Guardian Angel treasure, sent from above to teach and inspire Thomas how to love abundantly. This love has no bounds and is eternal.

Thomas and DiAnnie pray to God it will bring others and couples together in a way that they will understand miraculously, far beyond our comprehension or imagination.

There is a perfect love between a man and a woman. No matter how far down the scale they have gone.

Experience God's love, as vast as the universe, and grows towards this love between a man and a woman. John 15: 13. *Greater love hath no man than this, that a man lay down his life for his friends.* Romans 5: 5. *And hope maketh not ashamed; because the love of God is shed abroad in our hearts by the Holy Ghost which is given unto us.*

There is no other romance like it, experiencing a love that is far beyond human comprehension or imagination. Experience the miracles of biblical proportion and the near-death experiences that bring a life-changing eternal outlook.

Revitalize a relationship or marriage from the love that is eternal, experience love in a new way.

Be nice yourself because you're worth it. Thomas is proud of this guardian angel treasure and thanks God profusely daily.

Staying in that moment, everything is okay. This last-minute is gone; the next one is not here yet. The best revenge against regrets is forgiveness of self. The best revenge against resentments is the forgiveness of others. No regrets, no resentments, no matter how hard we try, we cannot turn the clock back.

Thomas does not take himself too seriously, not letting people, places, or things rent space in his head, including himself, only room for you and God.

Depression lies ahead of you if you are looking back to recapture the experience that will haunt you like a bad dream.

One moment of stress or worry is a moment of happiness you will never get back.

God's gift to us his life, what we choose to do with this life, is our gift to God.

CHAPTER 1

Soulmate Prayer From God's Grace

Everyone longs to give themselves completely to someone. To have a deep soul relationship with another, to be loved thoroughly and exclusively. Romans 5; 8. But God commendeth his love toward us, in that, while we were yet sinners, Christ died for us.

But God to the Christian says, "No, not until you're satisfied and fulfilled and content with living, loved by Me alone and giving yourself totally and unreservedly to Me, to have an intensely personal and unique relationship with Me alone.

"I love you, My child, and until you discover that only in Me is your satisfaction to be found, you will not be capable of the perfect human relationship that I have planned for you. You will never be united with another until you are united with Me—exclusive of anyone or anything else, exclusive of any other desires or belongings.

"I want you to stop planning, stop wishing, and allow Me to bring it to you. You keep watching Me, expecting the most significant things. Keep learning and listening to the things I tell you. You must wait.

"Don't be anxious, and don't worry. Don't look around at the things you think you want. Just keep looking off and away up to Me, or you'll miss what I have to show you.

"And then, when you're ready, I'll surprise you with love far more beautiful than any you would ever dream. You see, until you are prepared and until the one I have for you is ready, I am working this minute to have both of you organized at the same time. And until you are both satisfied exclusively with Me and the life I've prepared for you, you won't be able to experience the love that exemplifies your relationship with Me, and this is perfect love.

"And dear one, I want you to have this most wonderful love. I want you to see in the flesh a picture of your relationship with Me and to enjoy materially and concretely the everlasting union of beauty and perfection and love that I offer you with Myself. Know I love you. I am God Almighty. Believe and be satisfied."

1 CORINTHIANS 13:4-8

Love is patient and kind; love is not jealous or boastful; it is not arrogant or rude. Love does not insist on its way; it is not irritable or resentful; it does not rejoice at wrong but rejoices in the right. Love bears all things, believes all things, hopes all things, endures all things. Love never ends. AMEN

1 Corinthians 7: 2. *Nevertheless, to avoid fornication, let every man have his own wife, and let every woman have her own husband.*

You know you're in love when the hardest thing to do is say goodbye. If you love someone, tell them because hearts are often broken by words left unspoken. Alter your attitude, and you can alter your life. With love, Thomas prays from his heart that the forgiveness he asks for is God's will. I am the light says the Lord. He who follows me will never be in darkness. Thomas loves you, Jesus Christ!

Ephesian 3:20, Concentrate on the first sentence......*"The will of God will never take you where the Grace of God will not protect you."* Something Goodwill happens to you today—something that you have been waiting to hear. That is my prayer for you today.

For the souls who never thought that God could or would work in our lives, those who pray together stay together. Thomas is a Christian and only through the Grace of God and praise the Lord for that.

Perfection is a set-up for disappointment. This is not the Garden of Eden, and everything happens for a reason; giving and receiving is a two-way street.

From every human being, there rises a light that reaches straight to heaven, and when two souls that are destined to find each other together, their streams of light flowed together, and a single brighter light goes forth from there. United being. You were born together, and together you shall be forever, says the Lord.

1 Corinthians 7: 10. *And unto the married I command, yet not I, but the Lord, Let not the wife depart from her husband.*

That is God; he talks to us through the Holy Spirit. It is not how much you know but what you can do that count. God can do for us what we cannot do for ourselves. Thomas has brought souls through hell with him. God's not finished with Thomas yet. He has a past reckoning to make amends too. A spiritual feeling of the past destiny to rectify. (Revelation 3:3, *"Remember, therefore, what you have received and heard; obey it, and repent. But if you do not wake up, I will come like a thief, and you will not know at what time I will come to you."*)

I said a prayer for you today and know God must have heard; I felt the answer in my heart, although He spoke no word. I asked for happiness for you in all things great and small, but it was for his loving care that I prayed for most of all.

A caring heart. Any time I think of you, the one thing that I do is thank the Lord, and then I say a little prayer for you. I ask him to watch over you whenever we're apart, but most of all, I thank him for your kind and caring heart.

Don't quit when trials come, and things go wrong. When hardships lasted a bit too long, if you need help, ask for it, but don't give up, and don't you quit. Don't think about what might have been. When you're knocked down, get up again, they give yourself a talking to; believe those who believe in you. When are you tempted to admit that it'd be easier to quit? Instead of quitting, why not give it everything you've got? Don't give up, and don't give in. That's the way you're sure to win. Persevere and stick with it. You'll succeed if you don't quit!

Thinking of you, not to bring you fame or wealth or treasure, serve God's love as a reminder that you are cherished beyond measure. When you journey through your days, knowing God's love will never cease. Your path glows brightly, filled with an abundance of sunshine in your heart and filled with peace. Take your special spiritual gift carried within your soul, and when You Doubt Your Way, God's love will be your guide. The Holy Spirit will help remind you from sunrise until dark God holds you in his loving arms and keeps you near to his heart.

You say; it's impossible. God says; all things are possible

Luke 18: 27. *And he said. The things which are impossible with men are possible with God.*

You say I'm too tired. God says; I will give you rest.

Matthew 11: 28–30. *Come unto me, all ye that labor and are heavily laden, and I will give you rest. ²⁹Take my yoke upon you, and learn from me; for I am meek and lowly in heart, and ye shall find rest unto your souls. ³⁰For my yoke is easy, and my burden is light.*

You say I can't figure this out. God says; I will direct you. Proverbs 3: 5-6. *Trust in the Lord with all thine heart; and lean not unto thine own understanding. ⁶In all thy ways acknowledge him, and he shall direct thy paths.*

You say I can't go on. God says; my grace is sufficient.

2 Corinthians 12:9. *And he said unto me. My grace is sufficient for thee, for my strength is made perfect in weakness. Most gladly, therefore, will I rather glory in my infirmities than the power of Christ may rest upon me.*

You say I can't do it. God says; you can do all things.

Philippians 4: 9. *Those things that ye have both learned, received heard, and seen in me do; the grace of peace shall be with you.*

You say I'm not able to. God says; I am able.

2 Corinthians 9: 8. *And God can make all grace abound toward you; that ye, always having all sufficiency in all things, may abound to every good work.*

You say; it's not worth it. God says; it will be worth it.

Romans 8. *And we know that all good things work together for good to them that love God, to them who are the called according to his purpose.*

You say I can't forgive myself. God says; I forgive you.

1 John 9. *If we confess our sins, he is faithful and forgives us our sins and cleanse us from all unrighteousness.*

You say I can't manage. God says; I'll supply all your needs.

Philippians 4: 19. *Those things, which ye have both learned, and received, and heard, and seen in me, due; and the God of peace shall be with you.*

You say I'm afraid. God says; I'm not giving you fear.

2 Timothy 1: 2. *Two Timothy, my dearly beloved son; grace, mercy, and peace, from God the Father and Christ Jesus our Lord.*

You say I'm worried. God says, cast all your cares on me.

1 Peter 5: 7. *Casting all your care upon him, for he cares for you.*

You tell me I'm not smart. God says; I will give you wisdom.

1 Corinthians 1: 30. *But of him are ye in Christ Jesus, will of God is made unto us wisdom, and righteousness, and sanctification, and redemption.*

CHAPTER 2

God's precious grace, Christmas Eve

Thomas wrote;

The lifelong prayer Thomas has said, I find myself attracted to you. I'm madly in love with you. I love you so much, with such a magnetic passion, that it makes my heart hurt.

Your sweetness is unsurpassable by candies, and flowers cannot compete with your fragrance and beauty. Thank you for being real, honest, and trustworthy. I love you beyond words. Every day I'm drawn one step deeper in love.

I will never grow weary of being with you. My sweet, precious heavenly angel, I will always love you. You took my breath away the first time I looked into your heart and realized that you are one beautiful lady sent from above as one unique spirit. There's nothing single about being together with you. With you, tomorrow is inevitable.

When we are together tenderly kissing, I love you dearly, creating lasting and unforgettable memories. Together we have a unique love. Much more I desire to partake of with you today and forever. I will cherish you forever.

Before I met you, my angel, my life was miserable, and now I have the God-given opportunity to make up for those lost years by spending and to cherish every moment with you. I love you so much. 2 Corinthians 2: 4. *For out of much affliction and anguish of heart I wrote unto you with many tears; not that ye should be grieved, but that ye might know the love which I have more abundantly unto you.*

There's no law, time, reason, or idea holding back my secure love for you. I do not have any restrictions. I love you so much, only through God's precious grace, more than you could ever imagine. You mean everything to me. Proceeding forward with love for you, I've found happiness, joy, peace, and contentment.

Some say love hurts, but I will be glad to take any risk to be with you. I want to spend all my time with you. I can't envision what my life would be like without you. I love you dearly.

With you, I feel glorious and excellent. You and I are indeed meant to be. I love you beyond words. I fell in love with you even before I finally got the chance to meet you, before our eyes met, but I'm so glad that I did. I will love you, my precious angel, softly, tenderly, and gently with care and sensual compassion.

I loved you, and I will always securely love you and care for our love. I will cherish you forever. Only with me will you feel safe. There's nothing impossible about my goals and aspirations. I love you tenderly, sweetheart. Because of the electricity of our love, you'll never want or starve of the spiritual fulfilling a love.

2 Corinthians 13: 11. *Finally, brethren, farewell. Be perfect, be of good comfort, be of one mind, live in peace; and the God of love and peace shall be with you.*

No matter how problematic a day might be, it is a moment of happiness we will never get back. The thought of you always makes my day worth it. I love you so much. Whenever we are together, nothing else matters but you and me. I love you beyond the stars, into the light of eternal heaven. I wish I would have met you sooner. Then I could have loved you longer.

Three matches one by one struck in the night. The first to see your face in its entirety. The second to see your eyes. The last to see your mouth. And the darkness all around to remind me of all these. As I hold you in my arms.

Ephesians 4: 2. *That Christ may dwell in your hearts by faith; that ye, being rooted and grounded in love.*

Ecclesiastes 4: 9–12. *"Two are better than one because they have a good return for their labor: If either of them falls, one can help the other up. But pity anyone who falls and has no one to help them up. Also, if two lies down together, they will keep warm. But how can one keep warm alone? Though one may be overpowered, two can defend themselves. A cord of three strands is not quickly broken."*

Proverbs 31: 10-12. *"A wife of noble character who can find? She is worth far more than rubies. Her husband has full confidence in her and lacks nothing of value. She brings him good, not harm, all the days of her life."*

CHAPTER 3

The Vasectomy Reversal

Thomas and DiAnnie, praying to God, both knew instantly, and there was no hesitation that they were going to have children together. Through the grace of God, their faith and prayers together decided without a doubt to go forward. Thomas continuously updated DiAnnie on every minute, every moment of the procedure, the surgeon, the hospital, etc. This love is called agape.

Divine love is only given through the grace of God. This love has no beginning or no end; Thomas and DiAnnie have come together specifically for this love. And they pray to God that others in similar situations, through these writings, God willing, answer their prayers.

God's timing is impeccable and precise, a miracle or perchance? At this time, the executive branch of the government was authorizing sex changes throughout the military. Immoral an abomination against God, Thomas and DiAnnie looked at this as an opportunity to proceed forward with the vasectomy reversal.

Thomas reading and hearing on the national news media that military personnel had sex changes for taxpayers' cost of $90,000. Thomas wrote approximately a dozen letters and sent them out to different agencies within the Veterans Administration hospital. And he stated that he would pursue this with enthusiasm if they disagreed with this vasectomy reversal.

They receive a reply from the Veterans Administration, giving Thomas *permission to go ahead with the vasectomy reversal.* Thomas schedules an appointment with a highly qualified surgeon to perform the surgery. At the world-renowned hospital and school of medicine. And Thomas has never felt complete spiritually, after having a vasectomy.

Thomas, Notified almost immediately by the hospital and the doctor of the scheduled appointment for surgery. Thomas's surgery is planned for 2018, the year of our Lord. Thomas's date was at 4 AM.

The procedure of a vasectomy reversal is to place a small incision on each side of both testicles. And reconnect the tubes that produce sperm, once cut and tied. The doctor informed Thomas that he could come back and have another surgery until they were successful if it was not successful. The doctor almost gave Thomas 100% assurance that he would be able to father a child with DiAnnie.

After waking up from surgery, the medical staff informed Thomas that he could not do any lifting or any strenuous exercise for three months. Thomas's chances of getting his wife DiAnnie pregnant increase significantly after having this procedure done.

The feeling that Thomas had an immediate sense of spiritual satisfaction and completion. Recalling having his vasectomy how he felt spiritually, not like a man anymore, there was something mentally that was missing from his soul.

The feeling that Thomas had, was an instant feeling of spiritual satisfaction and completion.

CHAPTER 4

Death Row for the Unborn

Ironic and sad that Planned Parenthood accepts a woman's abortion in the state of Arizona. A girl under 18 years of age, without informing the parents, may go ahead and get an abortion. The mothers aborted sixty million babies in the United States last year alone for one reason or another.

This is death row for babies, as soon one of 6 million sperm cells make contact with that egg it is a life, a precious soul created by God and a divine creation. There never has been this divine creation, and there will never be another, unfortunately death row for the unborn, and God is watching. Not one omen owed to God shall go unpaid. This is an abomination against God, and tears of the Angels will not go unnoticed by God.

Matthew 5: 21. *Ye have heard that it was said by them of old time, Thou shalt not kill; and whosoever shall kill shall be in danger of the judgment.* Exodus 20: 13. *Thou shalt not kill.*

According to the American Census Bureau, 80% of American families grow up without a father figure. 70% of men in prison grew up without a father in the household. 50% of rapists grew up without a father figure in the family. Where these children go for love? Drugs, prostitution, and gangs. If God does not judge the United States of America, God will have to forgive Sodom and Gomorrah.

When Thomas arrived, it was kind of stunning that there were about eight young girls; only two of them had their mothers with them. Thomas was unaware of what these young ladies were in the hospital for, at first, until he asked one of them. She appeared to be under 18 years of age by herself. She then informed Thomas that she was there for an abortion.

One of the young ladies with a couple of her friends was crying, "Did not want to go through with the surgery of having an abortion." Thomas looking around, could not believe what he was seeing. Thomas felt like standing up and saying to all these young ladies, "please have these babies, and I will take care of all of them."

It was not appropriate timing to do or say anything to these young ladies. Most of them looked frightened. Thomas could tell all of them were terrified. One young girl with her mother, as well as another young girl, profusely crying. The other young ladies were just by themselves or with friends about their age. Thomas could only have to imagine the circumstances as to why they were getting an abortion.

This left a mark on Thomas's soul that he will never forget and always remember. The blood of these precious souls are crying out to God. The doctors and staff who partake in this precious life of all these angels will be held accountable for their participation.

This is like death row for the unborn. How can a society agree to such mayhem? These precious souls could have been something great in the eyes of God, another Albert Einstein, another Mother Teresa or the next president of the United States, only God knows.

Some of these young ladies were molested by their fathers or stepfathers, or relatives in the family. Maybe the boyfriends that got them pregnant did not want anything to do with it and asked them to please get an abortion. And possibly some of these young ladies were raped. Whatever the reason, this is an abomination against God.

There is no reason when you fall that you cannot get back up and keep on going, no matter what the circumstances. And there may be a tiny percentage as to why it would be appropriate for an abortion, the mother's health, molested by a stranger under criminal circumstances.

Some mothers want to abort this precious child of God's for evil possession for one reason or another. There are as many couples out there looking for babies that cannot have children. Thomas and DiAnnie have decided to devote their time, God willing, providing help for these young mothers and couples who would care to have a child of God.

One does not hear of vasectomy reversal that often or even on the news media, although when it comes to young lady's abortion, the whole world is aware of it, and laws are changed and passed. Thomas and DiAnnie feel that this is an injustice against society, but these young ladies are made to feel guilty for having an abortion.

And nothing is said when the man gets a vasectomy? It is the same thing, and one difference is that the world is run by male dominance over females. Keep one thing in mind, God is watching, and God is listening.

Thomas still cannot get this one out of his mind when Thomas was in the hospital, with those ten beautiful young ladies between the ages of 14 years old and 17 years old. A couple of them with their mothers most of them were by themselves.

Some of them looked like they were crying because their boyfriend or whoever raped them would not marry them take care of them.

And that feeling Thomas had, that could only come from being in that situation, of telling everyone of those young ladies to go ahead and have that baby I will take care of them.

Thomas put this on Facebook or something similar to this what he is saying above, and Thomas had an overwhelming response of people who wanted to donate-to a sanctuary of hope where these young girls can go and have their babies.

Thomas and DiAnnie are not sure if having a baby would be a good idea; they feel adopting them to start a home for unwanted mothers to have their children and show and provide for them love and respect.

It would be a great thing to do for a man to have a woman as his friend with him. Thomas cannot understand how abused and mistreated these young ladies are, an uneducated either they have mothers at home, and never show them love or rejected them.

The father's, stepfather, or some close family relative either abused them or raped them and never cared for these precious young girls or show them love either. Thomas gets this sick feeling in his stomach every time he thinks of men who will not care for a lady.

And Thomas is ready to do it all over again, only this time taking as many children as Thomas and DiAnnie can, and show them love and respect. Just thinking out loud, God bless with faith, love, and prayers.

DiAnnie's mother, Anna, is overwhelmed with joy and happiness and thanks to God continuously for this man that came into her daughter's life. Only through the grace of God, Anna recognizes this by her faith and prayers. Anna gives praise to God that she may one day finally become a grandmother. Thomas says to DiAnnie to tell her mother, Anna, "careful what you pray for; you just might get it." Smile.

Postscript; can you imagine Thomas and DiAnnie having two children, those two children having six children each. Thomas and DiAnnie's children will be calling their grandmother, Anna, for assistance with their children.

CHAPTER 5

Romantic Memoirs from Heaven

October 2018

1 October 2018

Thomas wrote;

Good evening sweetheart, I pray things are going well for you? I will always love you, so young beautiful you have submitted a change in love in me that will be eternal. For that, I thank God for you in my life. I spiritually feel that your dad and my dad have us together on some spiritual level. And all the miraculous characteristics we have in common. I certainly would appreciate a telephone call from you; I'm not sure what's going on in your life, other than you are busy and working hard. I am working very hard with many other people, God willing, for that, I would appreciate your prayers and your mother's.

A gift was given from God, I will always love you, and I will always be here for you when you need to talk to someone. I pray to God that you understand that Jesus said a house divided amongst itself would not stand. Mark 3; 25. And if the house be divided against itself, that house cannot stand.

Anyway, honey, until I hear from you, I will assume everything is okay and going well in your life. You're still my girl, and I'm still in love with you, and I love you hugs and kisses.

I'm not sure if you heard our conversation on the telephone, but I was directing Brian to wash clothes; I said take the clothes out of the washer that already cleaned, placed them in the dryer please, and picked up the few towels, and old clothes. I had them on our bedroom floor and put them in the washing machine.

That was the conversation we were having when I was on the telephone with you. I'm not sure if you heard any of it. If you did, you must have been laughing. I have to go in, start the washer and the dryer, and I will let you know, a simple task such as that, brother Brian has messed up, to be continued, smile.

DiAnnie, I'm not sure how you feel about me? I would not blame you if you found a good man that could take care of you and treat you better than I do. That does not change how I feel about you, and never will; you'll always be my girl. I will always be in love with you. No matter where you are or who you are with, you consume my every thought.

And the way I feel when I say words to you that I should not say makes me feel so bad about myself. I say to myself, let this beautiful young angel go, you are only hurting her unnecessarily, and she does not deserve that.

I would give my life for you, DiAnnie, which means if I have to let you go, I will be honest. John 15; 13. Greater love has no man than this that a man laid down his life for his friends. It will hurt my feelings and break my heart as it has never been broken before.

I'm not sure if I can get over that because I have not felt the love I have for you, so please do not feel wrong about anything. You are a precious angel in the eyes of God, and this is the way I have to think of you. With that radiant smile that can only come from God. In the few pictures I have seen of you, that bright smile makes me know in my heart that you are from heaven. Do not ever think I do not have work to do, and I do not have a clock to work from as you do.

A lady I went to a high school called me crying that her father just passed away. He was a good friend of mine, 98 years old and for his age doing very well. Two things none of us are getting out of this life without being called home and everyone will stand at the judgment seat in front of Jesus Christ our Lord.

It's a transition, and God will put the gold back into the fire to refine it and make it pure. For this reason, we must accept our trials and tribulations as a blessing. Even if that means suffering before we are qualified to get into heaven, and some people are so evil they never will get into heaven.

One thing, sweetheart, I have never wasted a moment of my life; I have done many not very good things, although never anything that I would call evil. I always had fun and laughed, and sometimes it was that others expense, and that's what I feel sorry about. I pray to God continuously for you and your mother and everybody that I know who could use some prayer, including myself.

I also mentioned that I saw a pregnant lady when Brian and I stop on our way to pick up the mail. She was about seven months pregnant and was chasing her little two-year-old son around, chasing him and holding him in her arms, and he was holding onto her. That reminded me of us, and especially you, the radiant glow that a lady has when she is pregnant is unexplainable.

You know it is a miracle from God, and seeing her loving that two-year-old boy and that little boy loving his mother right back. It reminded me of you and our love together that we may experience one day. I love you so much, and I will send this email now. I pray to God that you do not get upset or angry because I have more time than you do. Even though I should be working, you are my priority in life, and I love you so much sweetheart, hugs and kisses.

Once again, I said some not very nice words to you, one question I have, of all the men in this world, why did you pick a poor artist? A writer with nothing, a smile. I know it is not funny if you are still interested in me; things will get better for us, sweetheart. Have faith in God, and things will be okay. Unfortunately, I am not of this world, and I store all my riches in heaven. Luke 12: 21. So is he that lays up treasure for himself and is not rich towards God.

I realize that it is hard for a lady, a beautiful lady such as yourself, to understand. I have the faith that God will bless us, and we will never want for anything, as long as we have each other. God puts a soulmate in my life, and she is drawn to me for a Godly spiritual reason, and I'm so poor I cannot even pay attention, smile, and that's not funny.

I'm in love with you, you are all I ever think of, and that will never change. I have never felt the love like I believe in you, ever. I have never experienced this love that is

17

a God-given gift only through God's grace, and it is a miracle. I look at your pictures, and I have looked at other ladies' portraits. I have never seen a spiritual smile and glow of a radiance that could only come from God.

An angel sent from heaven into my life; look at a picture of yourself compared to any other of your girlfriends who are with you. You will see something unique about you in that picture together with your mother, which is precious. A God sent of complete happiness and joy, I will send this now to you, and I will write another email to you; I'm in love with you, my girl DiAnnie and that will never end, and things will get better please hang on sweetheart, hugs, and kisses.

2 October,

Thomas wrote;

The greater the storm, the greater the rewards, a sermon I was listening to about Moses, who was royalty in the King's court until he killed a slave then hid in the desert for 40 years. God came to him and said, go back and save my people. Moses on Mount Sinai was able to see God face-to-face receiving the 10 Commandments.

Joseph, his brothers sold him into slavery, ended up in the governor high priest, his wife made a pass at him. The Gov. placed Joseph in confinement. The governor knew that Joseph did not do it, and he liked Joseph. God came to Joseph in a dream to interpret the Pharaoh's dream. After seven years in prison, the cupbearer recalled that Joseph could interpret dreams.

The cupbearer mentioned to the feral about Joseph and his ability to decipher dreams. Joseph was brought forth out of prison standing in front of the Pharaoh. The Pharaoh's dream was, "the Pharaoh dream was, seventh in skinny cows came up out of the Nile River and consumed seven healthy cows.

Joseph was able to interpret the Pharaoh's dream, seven years of the harvest to save, for the seven years of famine to follow. And Joseph became second in command next to the Pharaoh. And that's where Joseph met his 11 brothers, who did not know it was Joseph until he showed him that he was circumcised.

Sometimes the greatest reward is coming through the tremendous storm, and we all have trials to go through in this life. My faith is unshakable, and I am going through a great storm right now, and God has let me know that coming out the other side of the storm, I will be blessed.

One thing while I am thinking of it, those two books I sent you, they are going to be worth blessings you cannot count one day. So keep them for your children as well as yourself. The miracles that I have experienced in my life are far beyond my comprehension. Has only strengthened my faith in God through Jesus Christ, our Lord's name amen. Jesus walked on water after the apostles had slept and were awakened by a severe storm. And Jesus said, fear not to be of great joy, and the apostles thought, who is this that can calm the seas? There's so much I would like to say to you and so little time for my love for you. I cannot express myself in a lifetime the love that I have for you.

Keep these words in your heart and never let them tear us apart, even if you are with another soul. These words will console you in troubled times of the storms. Grace and peace of the Lord be with you, as my thoughts of my heart go forward with you, in love and compassion to never be forgotten.

We will be together again one day, possibly not here on this earth, eternally in heaven for sure. Through Jesus Christ our Lord, and with God, all the angels, and saints, there we will be for eternity. I have always loved you, I am in love with you, and I will never stop loving you. You are my girl, hugs, and kisses.

Everybody else is doing it. Money can buy you amusement but not happiness, money can buy the best doctors, but only God can heal you, money can buy you the best food, but only God can give you the appetite to enjoy it, money can buy you a house, but not a home. Happiness is sitting on your back porch, watching your children and grandchildren screaming all around you. There are two types of people in this world, those who bow down to everything in it as their God or those who bow down to Jesus Christ to get to God. John 6; 44. No man can come to me, except the father who has sent me to draw him, and I will raise him at the last day. No one comes to the father but by me says Jesus Christ our Lord and Savior.

The best things in life are free; since Jesus Christ arrived on the scene, they wanted to kill him, and he went to the cross for our sins and resurrected three days later 13 different locations and over 500 people witnessed the resurrection of Jesus Christ.

King Nebuchadnezzar was thrown in the fire; the fire was seven times hotter than expected. The fire consumed the people that threw them into the fire. It was so hot.

The King said I thought we threw those three Hebrew children into the fire? I see four of them, which look like their God and Savior of the universe. They were unbound and walking around in the fire. And they came out without even a single mark.

Adam and Eve were offered the whole orchard, and God gave them one command not to eat from the tree of good and evil. And they only took one bite of the forbidden fruit, only one time. These are sermons I have watched, and I'm still watching today. I thought they were fascinating. And I pass this on to the one I care for, which will pass this on to her children one day.

Because this beautiful young lady named DiAnnie will indeed have children one day and grandchildren as well, and rightfully so, pass this on and pray with them together, understanding that the brevity of life is but a twinkle of an eye. It seems to be the older you get, the faster it goes, and this I know. So I do not wait. That is a waste of life for me at this point. Your children can have something to remember a man you once knew.

To this man, his faith was unshakable, and the miracles were abundant, and this man is in love with this lady always has been and always will be. Hugs and kisses.

Postscript; this God-given gift of a lady has crossed this man's path and was touched by an Angel. That brought him out of the fiery depths of hell and put him through the refining fire so that he can reap the harvest of God's kingdom through Jesus Christ our Lord's name amen.

4 October 2018

DiAnnie wrote

Hello sweetheart,

It has been a few days since you heard from me. I have been in the hospital again for my knees since I got back to The North Country. I feel a bit better now; praise the Lord! How have you been keeping as well? I hope that you're blessed. I hate when I keep silent *from you, but I had no choice because the pain becomes unbearable, and I don't think straight unless I take morphine.*

I have read all your lovely messages, and believe me, and it feels great doing that. You're right, my love, I too, feel our meeting is never perchance but something that was meant to be. Before we were born, the destiny was already set; God never makes a mistake because He knows now, later and tomorrow,

Thomas wrote;

Respect him; when you told me that your mother said that, that said to me that your mother was close to God. That is a Bible verse. 1 Peter 3; 1. Likewise, you wives, be in subjection to your husbands; that, if any obey not the word, they also may without the word be one by the conversation of their wives. James 2; 1. My brethren have not the faith of our Lord Jesus Christ, the Lord of glory, with persons' respect. Jesus Christ our Lord our God the father, and for that, can you please forgive me?

When I say something to you that is mean, I learn a whole volume about doing the right thing, and you are my teacher. And for the grace of God, only knows why you have stayed with me this long. You are my guardian angel, and if it were not for you, I would not be going to heaven.

You are so precious in my eyes. Keep in mind that I have been living alone for years and have talked to many other ladies. And I will never compare them with you, although in my mind there might be one word you say that tells me for a moment, I may be talking to one of those ladies.

And you are so precious in my eyes. I love you so much, and you were a heaven-sent from God. Writing me that first long email, and that's when I start praying to God, God, are you kidding me?

And you work so hard, and I pray to God one day when the Spirit moves you, that you can give up your job, your friends, for our marriage and our children.

God will bless us beyond measure with my unshakable faith and your prayers behind me, and your respect for me. You have to believe me when I say that I have experienced too many miracles in my life. And you are the most precious and beautiful miracle I have ever experienced in my life. I have never known a love that we have between us. You must realize that I will take care of you, I will love you, we will laugh together, we will have children together, we will be happy, joyous, and free.

God will be with us through Jesus Christ, our Lord's name, we believe, and we have the faith. Jesus went to the cross for our sins and our past evil deeds. They have been forgiven. When you get it in your mind to come to our home and live together, please do not hesitate to let me know, but make sure that is what you want to do.

If for any reason it is not, please do not let me believe any different, I will treat you with respect, and God will bless us with everything we need.

God knows the answer to our prayers and our needs before we even ask. Everything will be okay. You are my girl, I am in love with you, and I love you.

So whatever you decide to leave Montréal, quit working, and let go of your friends to have a family and grandchildren for your mother. Please let me know as soon as possible. Waiting is a waste of life, and if you love me the way that I feel, you do. You will not hesitate, and the Holy Spirit of God will let you know exactly what to do. And it will feel okay, and everything is going to be okay.

You can read this email to your mother and with both of your prayers that are very powerful throughout all of our lives. It is like I had met you before, when your mother said, "respect him," she heard something in your voice or saw something in your eyes. That your mother, with her intuitive wisdom, noticed that I was the man to be in your life and to have our children together.

I spiritually feel this, and you can talk it over with your mother if you care. I would appreciate you doing that, and please forgive me for all the negatives bad things I have said to you.

2 John 1; 3. Grace be with you, mercy, and peace, from God the Father, and the Lord Jesus Christ, the father's son, in truth and love. Like I had mentioned, you are my teacher, spiritual guide, and Guardian Angel. Hugs and kisses.

8 October 2018

DiAnnie wrote;

Good morning sweetheart, hope that everything is going well with you, and as I woke up today, you were the first person on my mind, and I thought to message you and know how you're feeling. I was doing a lot better now from the migraine last night. I took meds and in better shape this morning on my way too short to work. I have seen all of your messages and missed calls. You said a few things that get me asking why you ask me these things sometimes, like being drunk and calling you the other night. I wasn't drunk at all. I was just tired and reading your messages. I didn't know how to respond and had to think for a while before getting back to you. You know it's easier for you to message several times a day since you only talk and the dragon app does the typing,

Sure my mom wants the best for me in life. That is why she encourages me to be respectful to you, we may have a love life, but you must respect me and me. My mom wants a caring person in my life, not an abusive person. She wants her grandkids' father to be a responsible man and calm, and I tell her you are a good man to me.

I heard you had gotten help already. I'm very concerned about you just how much you do for me. One thing I like about you is the fact you're never too big to realize your mistakes, that's a positive attitude, and I love you very much for that.

Why would I be killing myself? I know the friend you're talking about that contacted you is called Thomas! 😃. I appreciate it when you make my life each time! You're a silly Zoro that knows how to make your girl smile. Why do you ask me if I'm committed to you? You know I do, and you know that very much. I feel sad about you always repeating things. We have talked about this several times about coming to your home. I'm more interested in this because everyone here knows I'm in love with an Arizonan, so if I do not reach it would be like what they know already isn't true. Do you realize why I am interested more than what you think? You forget sometimes, and I'm not going to be mad because everyone does.

Can you do one thing for me? Please stop asking if I love you or how I feel about our love. We both love each other, so why do you try to be one-sided and asking questions like a person with doubts? What exactly I do that makes you ask me? Sure, I know there's power in the blood of Jesus! Without Him, who is stronger? No one, absolutely no one! Here thinking about you, I like you to know that you're always in my heart and prayers. My mom's prayers for me as well.

Thanks so much for all the messages. I'll call you later when I'm back home. Enjoy the rest of your day, handsome. Warm hugs 😬 and kisses 😙 From your endless love 🤍

Thomas wrote;.

How can I talk about our goals without making you feel like you are being pressured? And taking me away from my thoughts of our dreams together? I will admit they are not always God's thoughts. For that, I accept full responsibility.

I cannot help myself from being consumed by our presence together. That beautiful will not change, I don't think, and I'm not sure if I would want it to? Through my faults, you teach me, and I am a fast learner, not since our communication until this point. I feel I have changed for the better only because of you, and a lot of that came through my thinking about our goals together. Help me? I'm drowning, I'm not sure if I should smile, but I think I will, whether you like it or not, so take that, my beautiful girl.

I may have to get into intense fellowship with my girl again, with all of you, and just me, oh my, what shall I do? I am outnumbered beyond human comprehension, yet, I am willing to throw myself into the ring with my girl DiAnnie. With all of her cohorts, triple smile.

I would also like to ask you, my sweetheart, my beautiful little precious DiAnnie, if I believe you mentioned that I was jealous of you, did I read that incorrectly?

I'm not sure if I would agree with you on that. What I have said on numerous occasions, all I want is your happiness and freedom in life, and that in itself means everything.

Do you recall the time that we went on a hike together to the beautiful countryside? And we each had our backpacks on when all of a sudden we came upon a bear. And you drop to the ground immediately, pulling a pair of sneakers out of your backpack and putting them on rapidly. And I said, "DiAnnie, you cannot outrun that bear! And you replied, "I do not have to outrun that bear. All I have to do is outrun you.

I would give my life for you, and you witness that when you drop down to put on your sneakers, I said to run my beautiful DiAnnie, run fast, this is the unrevealing reason God had us bring our sneakers along. We had no idea we were going to encounter trouble ahead. God did! Smile, all you do is make me smile. I can't help smiling. Sometimes I cannot stop, and that, my sweetheart, I can blame exclusively on you— quadruple smile.

Have a good night, honey. A drilling task, a labor of love, my sweet, beautiful love, hugs and kisses, and you can take those to the bank, smile.

DiAnnie wrote,

Hi sweetheart,

Thanks for keeping in touch with me. I appreciate all your messages. I'll reply much better tomorrow. I just wanted to let you know that I got all you wrote, and I not intentionally keeping silent. I love you so much and know you're my true love. My endless love and my Zoro. 😁📇

Thomas wrote;

Sweetheart, my precious girl, say the name soulmates to anyone in the conversation, watch their reaction. I have not heard back from you, and I was doing some dangerous thinking, you know me? Smile,

Brian lost my driver's license? Tomorrow should bring new light on the day, and pray God we will find it, say a prayer for us, please. You might ask, "how did brother Brian lose my driver's license? Brian not only misplaced my driver's license, a major credit card as well. Brian had them both in his possession. I will have Brian run errands for me, and he will need my credit card and my picture identification on my driver's license to purchase items.

We were at the Veterans Administration Hospital for an appointment. After I was finished with my appointment. I usually always drive my vehicle to the Veterans Administration hospital and back home. When Brian wheeled me up to the driver's seat, and I got into my car. Then Brian wheels might need a wheelchair to the hatchback of the vehicle. He opens it and places my chair inside the car, and closes the hatchback. Then, I just took off and was going to leave him there.

I proceeded to step on the gas and was about to drive off without him. As I look back into his face, he had the most ironic look on his face. And I'm serious. Even the angels in heaven would have had to have laughed. I cannot explain the look, but it made me laugh. Instead of just driving off and leaving him there, I had to stop and let him back into the vehicle.

I love you, and I'm in love with you; I always have been, and God most certainly knew that before either of us did. I know what I was going to mention to you. Also please, ask your mother for me, how fast time goes? No pressure is just a question. I want to get reconfirmed, and I would appreciate your feedback on that question. Her being a lady and your mother. It would mean a lot to me; let me put it this way, it would certainly be interesting, and if you do not think it is an appropriate question, do not ask; hugs and kisses.

9 October 2018

DiAnnie wrote;

Good morning honey, I hope you're having a good day; mine is going great so far. I woke up not too long ago. I read your messages and the book, and I realize a few things I need to talk about.

Anything you want in life for a benefit should be taken time off to handle well, whatever will live forever after we are not anymore, how will people digest it? Are we getting the best promotions? Let's consider important things so that our work will be admired. Let's not do it in a hurry. I hope you understand what I'm saying. Well, acting wouldn't be so bad, but it has not been my dream, but who knows life changes. I don't think I would want that because you have started being jealous of the guys in Hollywood already 😃 better I am a stay-at-home mom.

I felt terrible last night the way you answered me but, Think about all this. I'm on my way to work now. Have a good day! Love you 😎.

Thomas wrote;

Tell your friends or customers or whomever that you know someone who has written, and asked them what they think about the books? I feel it will be well worth the effort.

I'm tired of hurting your feelings, and I do not want to say the wrong things, but I will, being a man, and I'm not pressuring you or are getting together, whenever that happens, it will be God's will not ours.

I'm not kidding you when I told those two ladies the title of the book. They whipped out their pens and notepads immediately. They wrote that down with great interest, and their eyes were bugged out and wide open. I mentioned that it would be out within six months to a year, which did not bother them from writing the title down.

Hugs and kisses, double hugs and kisses, make sure and let your mother know my prayers are with her.

Thomas wrote;

I pray you understand my reasoning, and the decision will be yours, my sweet, beautiful girl, my precious Guardian Angel. Now I was thinking, and this is what I get for thinking, I am proposing, and it is only a suggestion. I do not say this to hurt your feelings. That we take our pictures. My reason being is that I'm not sure when you plan to come to Arizona or under what circumstances. Only God knows.

I doubt if either of us does, you more than likely do, but I'm clueless, and I know one person that knows, God our father.

Please advise me; in other words, I need your help sweetheart, I cannot do this without you, beautiful, the precious angel I am in love with. God loves both of us as well as your mother; hugs and kisses.

It would help if you did not feel pressure; I wouldn't say I like that feeling, and I do not care for anybody who puts anybody up against the wall to make a decision, especially a lifetime decision. It is a serious decision, and I realize that it's your decision, not my decision. I will never regret the two of us meeting, and the love we have for one another is from God. Hugs and kisses.

11 October at 6:37 AM

DiAnnie wrote;

Sorry for my delay. 🖋 ❤️ 😭 😀

Good morning sweetheart, I'm not intentionally keeping silent from you. You think wrongly about me sometimes, and it makes me feel less comfortable with that. I haven't been feeling well since I last talked to you on the phone and messaged you. I have a cold, and my voice is gone; I'm applying some pills, and I'm just getting better now.

We have talked repeatedly, but you do the same repetition each time; what do you expect me to do or say? You know that I'm always honest with you, and I have no reason to get angry.

You also said that I should tell you to continue your life if I don't want to keep in touch, another negative word from you. If I ever want to continue my life, I wouldn't be a coward; I'll tell you directly and not hide anything from you. I hope you understand that you make me sad with all those negative things you say.

You tell me that you don't let me feel pressured, but you do, so how do you think about something like that? I guess you got excellent ideas, and it makes sense to include our pictures and names. We don't have to be in a hurry. We must take our time so that we can do a good job. I hope you understand. You're always in our prayers, and believe me, not a day that you're not in our prayers.

You continually mention us in your prayers, and we wouldn't be heartless not to do so for such a loving person like you! My heart goes to you each day, and I think my schedule and life, for now, make it seems as if I show less concern for you.

Not so. I wish others would see inside of our hearts to know how much we care. Not possible right? But God knows the best of how much I care for this Zorro.

The only thing is this Zorro is too fast to make his girl feel sad; this is something not easy to take from you; your life as a former Marine has had a significant impact on you.

You are a loving person, not going to deny it, but you have another tough side of you. I wish you were a little Thomas to give some tough training to change from making me feel sad.

No worries, honey. I pray that God will restore our wants according to His glory so that we, as His children, will be happy. Never think I'll ever have you out of my life, and never feel that way; we may have our differences sometimes, but what is right in the hearts will always be there. Enjoy your day, and sorry for my silence. Love you very much, Mr.

12 October 2018

DiAnnie wrote;

Good morning sweetheart! I hope you're well doing great this morning, honey, and I have dreamed about us as you were Busy sending messages. I see why I kept dreaming 😄 they say dreams are real; I believe that now lol.

Now I can take my time to reply to your messages. First, I wanted to let you know that I did not say it was terrible to have served your country. I told you the military training made you a bit different from regular people. Not just you but anyone that has been a part of military-related work. That doesn't you're not a God-fearing guy, you're, and I know you're a loving person.

I wouldn't deny that at all. Most strict people are ordinarily good at heart; just people think what they see from their faces makes them like that. Such people believe deeply from the core, so don't feel I'm scared of this tough Marine lol I know he's the right person.

Well, I'm getting over the cold now, and believe me, it haves me hell. When I was at work, some people thought there was something wrong with me that I refused to talk lol, but I explained that to my boss. Your prayers help, and I appreciate that. You must have an excellent human system to be cold-proof, lol! I wish you could lend me your system! Do so if I had a cold and we slept in the same bed, wouldn't it be transmitted to you? Or when I kiss you several times?

Thanks always for putting us in your prayers, my mom and I; that is so sweet of you. We pray for you continually as well. With such caring hearts, we will surely be a great family. I continue to pray for you. I know nothing is too hard for God. Just put everything in His hands.

Loving each other and solving each other minor problems is better than dashing me with millions. That's not my life. I live a simple one because I have seen a bit of it and know what it means to live simple. I pray that our dreams and prayers will come to the past; the most important things to me are having our children, having a great future for them, and writing to win souls for Christ.

This doesn't mean along the way, there wouldn't be problems, but the way we will approach these problems will depend on whether we will fail or succeed. When all is done, and you're ready to send me a copy, just let me know.

Do you ask how long I will tie you up? Well, if I think you're not listening would be for hours, but when you hear, I wouldn't have to tie this guy I love so much. You think I hate you, right? You must be kidding. I love you very much, even with all you sometimes do. I'll get going, Mon Zorro, know that your Zoroette loves you very much! I catch you later this evening, okay. Kisses 😘 and hugs 🤗 Your endless love.

Thomas wrote;.

Sweetheart, I believe you misunderstand me. It is never about your body; I mean that it's not about love in a charming kind way. Our passion is much stronger and more meaningful than that. And I believe you realize that I hope and pray, it is a spiritual connection we have, and the love we have between us is far beyond our comprehension. God's love for one another is heaven-sent. From sky to sky, there is no end to our love for each other. The love that we will have for one another will help save many souls, marriages, and relationships. I genuinely believe this. And you are right, and this is who we are, and will always be, sweetheart.

Just a footnote; I went to the hospital this morning for my appointment to keep in mind this is the most significant and newest hospital in the world. Veterans come from all over the world to this hospital, and I feel very fortunate to live nearby.

My doctor, whom I have not seen for about six months, and was on his computer. I informed this Dr. Of the letters I have written. I was asking him if he had heard or received any information concerning the vasectomy reversal. He then asked me about that young lady in The North Country, if we are still going to get together?

I was surprised, so I feel all the staff in that colossal hospital knows why I am getting the vasectomy reversal. And proceeding forward with this unusual request, spiritually, I think that this medical facility and all the staff are aware of my request.

So it seems everyone knows about my girl from The North Country, through Dr. of whom is the only Dr. I have informed of our Godly intentions. Anyway, the medical profession is safe as far as information goes. I love you and miss you.

And you are right; I do have a lot of work to do today; I just got back from the hospital. It is 2 PM here, Arizona time. I will have more for you later. I had to see a social worker that I had met for the first time. She was a lady. Do we agree or disagree? I'm in love with you, sweetheart. You are my girl, and I love you. Make sure you let your mother know that my prayers are with her hugs and kisses.

15 October 2018

DiAnnie wrote;

Hi sweetheart,

I can finally write you now and head to bed later. I have been getting all your emails, and earlier, the call was messed up, so I just thought to write you a quick message. I hope you're still up. First, I'm glad that you're going to do the vasectomy surgery soon; it's our future, and also, my heart goes to you.

My advice is that you don't have to fear as long you know you're right.

Those judges are nothing but humans, and I like what you wrote there that you're going to tell the judge you're right to the point, and nothing much because it's the fact that you wrote just remember that and all will be fine.

I call my mom not too long, and she's praying for you as well. We never forget to mention you in prayers each day. You have a good heart, and you're a part of us, and whatever that concerns us as well.

Good that you tell them that we met somewhere. I do the same with my friends and others I talked to about knowing each other before exposing them. You came here, and I met you from the restaurant I work.

This way, no one can stick their noses in our affairs. People are fast to have their say but don't know how those involved feel about themselves. As long the two of us think the same way, it's the more we love each other.

I have wanted to ask how old is brother Brian? He forgets so fast, maybe poor memories, lol. I thought you said you were getting your driver's license the other day. If he put in for it by now, you have earned it, but you can find it hopefully.

I'm exhausted, and I'm up late tonight, so I'll go to get a shower and go to bed for tomorrow. It's always significant to hearing from you, my love. All my heart and prayers with you, I'll dream about us and will continually keep you in my prayers. Love you so much. Sweet dreams and kisses 😘.

16 October 2018

DiAnnie wrote;

Hi *honey,*

Sorry, and I hope you understand when it takes me a while to reply to you; please do that each time for my sake as we both are not on a similar schedule. If so, I don't think it would even take me a second to reply. I appreciate each time you understand the situation, and it tells me a lot about your heart and what kind of person you are. My day was busy as usual, thanks for asking.

Sure, I'm taking care of myself, but I believe it's not easy for a struggling girl who is all alone with no parental backing and having to survive as possible as I can. We keep you in prayers always, and I am a little worried about you. The truth must be the truth, but sometimes people are understood differently, and I realize that's what happened today.

We can speak the truth but shouldn't be judgemental as people will misunderstand your good gestures. You are just an upright person, and you get so nervous about humans' corruption as you see around us today.

Luke 6; 37. Judge not, and ye shall not be judged: condemn not, and ye shall not be condemned: forgive, and ye shall be forgiven.

Homosexuals are everywhere, and the Bible is against it, and you know unbelievers would not care less to understand you, so the best approach is moderate, that's all. I know all you said, and I think sending an email as the mature one is the best thing to do; you're a loving soul, and they know that just the situation was emotional, and they got things messed; I tell people always that the worst, and most dishonest people are lawyers, religious leaders, politicians, and financial institutions.

My question is, do you see things going your way with this case? Prayers are the answer. Don't be shaken. I know you're not the kind to be surprised. I pray that they will give what belongs to you and not try to punish you for any reason. The best person to turn to when situations are beyond our control is God. Like Thomas in the Bible, he wasn't much of a nice guy, but he always turns to God no matter what. He made God the center of his strength. I want you to know that our understanding is no more like those of the world after we are saved. So understand that there wouldn't be much agreement with such people whenever you're in a situation, be it, family or strangers.

Let's keep seeking God's direction. You have been a lady's man ever since childhood 😃 you have been a Zorro for your kid wife!

No wonder there's an extraordinary coincidence that I called you a Zorro, and then your dad's birthday is the same as mine. I think God knew we were going to meet one day! Sure this week is a hectic week for you, I prayers that all goes well. Thanks for getting back to me, and I know you're the one I'm thinking about each time. Enjoy your night, and lets God be our guide. Warm hugs and kisses 😘, and remember you're my Zorro!

Thomas wrote;

Peace and grace of our Lord and father be with you and your mother through Jesus Christ the Lord's name amen, please let your mother know that my prayers are with her.

I was looking over this social media form I believe I have emailed you a copy. They sent me a copy of the instructions, and this one I am taking my time with; it's going to be perfect, and it's going to be directed towards heaven. And the blessing from God Almighty and our prayers may finally be answered.

Like I have mentioned before, it would allow us to meet one another in person someday. And remember, when you bring a friend, get a Catholic nun with the big switch, triple backflip laughing, your mother may be a perfect chaperone.

Now keep in mind, you are finally teaching me how to treat a lady. And we are going to grow and love together eventually, more expansive than the universe, and a love beyond our comprehension that only God knows. Helping other souls, think about it, DiAnnie, isn't this a God-given gift and a miracle? And did it come together at the right time? I would just be thinking today and praying. Your mother and yourself must have been praying hard.

Like I mentioned before, please bring a friend; this is not a honeymoon vacation just yet. Big :-(, triple big sad face, with the big back to the smile.

Jude 1; 7. Even as Sodom and Gomorrha, and the cities about them in like manner, giving themselves over to fornication, and going after strange flesh, are set forth for an example, suffering the vengeance of eternal fire.

This will be, how shall we say, a rigorous working vacation with no breaks. So no hanky-panky, do not get fresh, do not put your hands on me, do not kiss me, you know what kissing leads to? The bedroom, smile we are not going there yet, if we have waited this long, we can wait a little longer, maybe.

I feel both of us would agree that if we passed up a blessing like this from God, we might as well go out in the backyard and tie ourselves up and leave ourselves there. Smiling,

I am getting ahead of myself into excited and slow down with patience, which is hard for me to do; I will make this social media page perfect. The only way I can do that is to let the Holy Spirit work through me and God's blessings through Jesus Christ our Lord's name, my girl and her mother's prayers if you have ever prayed for anything in your life, like winning the lottery.

Marrying a multibillionaire that is deaf, dumb, and blind 98 years old in a rocking chair, and you are young and beautiful, and he leaves his real estate to you before he kicks the bucket—smile like a Marine. I think the devil made me do that, and I do not believe that came from God. Although God does have a sense of humor, as you can see, one thing at a time, let me get this social media paper finalized, and I will email it to you, beautiful.

I pray to God if this happens, you will know better, you are far more intelligent than I am, and you know you. I will email you everything, all the social media hits, so you will know precisely when it's time to come to Arizona and start writing.

In other words, you will not be coming to Arizona to meet me to play hanky-panky; you will be coming to Arizona because you see a great opportunity.

Whether that opportunity includes us together, as married children of God, all of a sudden, everything is ruined, they throw all their morals out the windows, and all other character defects come out of them. They are from the devil, keeping that in mind.

I'm patiently applying myself with enthusiasm to this project, okay beautiful? Are you in the ballpark? Are you on the soccer field? Are you on the ski jump? Are you in the ice-skating rink? Are you in the ice hockey arena? Are you ice-skating? Are you ice fishing? Are you harpooning seals? Are you on a sled? Are you throwing snowballs? Are you building snowmen?

What is my little ZOROETTE doing? Are you sleeping at a time like this? LOL, triple smile with the double backflip, triple backflip hit the ground, front forward double flip with the half twist, and a full gainer, with a jackknife off the bed on the floor, another triple backflip over to the bed, bouncing off the bed, as I do it for forwarding kiss back to the desk, whatever forwards kiss means.

How can fun for a one-morning continuously bring happiness? Big hug, and don't tie me up when you get out here if the opportunity occurs. It may or may not, God willing, I will pray hard? I do mean pray hard and not with anger.

I usually use the word angry or upset or other cuss words, and you come up with a name like anger. That was funny when you said that, the great big giant smile.

I might call you on the telephone and wake you up. Then again, I might not. Brian and I are leaving at 8 AM to the Department of Motor Vehicles in Arizona to get my driver's license. A big happy note.

17 October 2018

DiAnnie wrote;

Good evening sweetheart, Glad I home after another busy day. It is always great to hear from you; reading your messages brings smiles to me, and I appreciate your efforts in staying in touch with me. How was your day today? I hope that everything went according to the way you wanted; life usually does not pleases us, being that it's how it was created.

You expect a result then what you expected does not come the way you want most of the time. But with God, we get along. You know, working with many people isn't easy, but I get along. I appreciate when you understand what I tell you and believe I do not feel any pressure at all, you bring out ideas, and as long they're right, I'll let you know. If not, I'll still let you know. We have a lot of work to do together from afar to achieve the first, and then we can accomplish a lot when we start to live together, so it's a test for our first work.

Whenever I read your messages and read all the prayers, concerns, and compliments, I realize how much you're a one in a kind among men. I can see your love and care and feel your protection; this way, the song you sent me, "Hero," tells many of your heroic abilities to protect the one you love. That's why I called you a Zorro. You're a hero in the way of all the sacrifices you made for your country as a Marine.

I also find you romantic, and when I'm reading your messages, I have that excitement in me that when we had loved. You'll genuinely take the hell out of me and makes me feel a deep romance. You're such a sweet person Thomas. Sure we have a lot in common, and our meeting isn't an accident. I realize many things that predestined that God truly made us for this, and I'm glad we can see it coming together for His glory, not ours. The fact that you're concern about my mom tells me a lot that you genuinely care for us, and I appreciate it.

I saw the covers of the book. The graphics are beautiful, and I think she is calm. I think about all those sweet words you tell me each time, and I got a tremendous feeling and have me all to yourself how I love you, honey! Enjoy your time, and I'll get a shower and sleep. I'm so so tired. Know that I'm thinking about you, sweetheart. Peace and prayers for you. From your arctic treasure! 😀 🍃 🔔 ♥ CA.

18 October 2018

DiAnnie wrote:

Hi sweet man, How's this handsome man doing?

I got a voicemail from you but not sure what it said as it's taking longer to load; I just got home not long ago and thought to check you out. I didn't hear from you today, and I'm assuming that you must've gone out to the hospital for the checkup. I hope that everything went tremendous or is going great. My heart goes to you each time and knows that you're loved very much. Let me know how you are doing. I'll keep playing your voicemail. For now, take care, and I'll see about dinner and get a shower and see about getting some rest. Take care of yourself, honey. Kisses and hugs 😬.

Thomas wrote;

Beautiful, keep in mind we are not alone, God loves his children, I'm going to write more in a minute maybe about 10 minutes have to answer all my telephone calls on the answering machine. I have some emails from my publisher I see, so I'm not sure when I will be back, I said 10 minutes it might be more the like half an hour to an hour I can hardly wait to write to you about everything, I pray your day went well and get some good sleep sweet dreams you are precious in my eyes xoxo.

Thomas wrote;

Peace and grace be with the Lord and you and your mother through Jesus Christ our Lord's name amen.

I have so much to say in the short time we have not talked; believe it or not, God has us both busy; I understand that it is hard for you to realize that I am busy with this much time to write you an email to this extent. As usual, here I am, a smile. I'm not sure where to start. Let me put this in some order.

Yesterday, I was absorbed not only with you but also with absorbing my mind with prayer, which I love, and that will not change. Then it was fasting in prayer, and sometimes we wonder if God is even listening. Well, He is in all His glory through His Son Jesus Christ, our Lord's name.

This morning started early and hectic I always like to get to where I'm going early. It shows common courtesy and respect for those that have held an appointment for you. I had simply a blast at the medical Center facility today, huge hospital people from all over the world. It is just like walking down Broadway or 34 Street in New York City, a fascinating mix of people. Once again, I am very blessed in that I live so close, and they are building and building like mad all over that Expanding renowned hospital facility.

Then we get on these little tram buses taking you from near your vehicle to where you're supposed to be going, with about 10 to 15 other people. And of course, you know me, smile in front of those people I accused the bus driver and the doorman who helps the people of pocketing the people's wallet as they get off and on the bus. Triple smile, as a result, I had everyone on the bus laughing in hysterics. Including Brian, he could not believe what I was saying, and it was just one life experience that I found to be spiritually really enlightening.

I brought joy into many people's lives; we were on the elevator with one man and his two boys. The boys were about eight years old and 11 years old. And the man said when he got off the elevator, thank you for serving our country, as I was wearing my Marine Corps vest as I always do. And I said, "I would like to thank you for not serving if you have not, as well as these young men here, for it gave us a reason to serve, and for that, I thank you."

Beautiful, I'm going to pick this up in another email. For a reason, I do not want to lose this one. I will be right back in about 15 minutes. I'm not getting any more times. Let us put it this way. I will be back excitingly looking forward to it because you absorb my mind with love and prayers. You're my girl.

Thomas wrote;

Beautiful, if this were the perfect world, we would have no use for God. Jesus Christ, his only son, our Lord, would not have to have come into this world to save us from our sins and our past. I have a spiritual feeling that you and I are connected in more ways than one in the short time you have been in this life on your own. We never walk alone, and there are times when we think we walk alone. More shall be revealed, and you do realize that don't you? Is a reason you are my girl, and I am your Zorro. I get God's thoughts, not think about this DiAnnie. You and I both say we have problems and issues presently and in our past.

Time is drawing near to an end in this world, and reading the Bible continuously in all my spare time and thinking of the two of you or us. Do we believe we are experienced difficulties now? There are many jealous people in this world, especially those who want what we have, including our friendship. You and I know we are equally yoked spiritually. Otherwise, God would not have dropped us off in each other's arms in a way that we find ourselves.

And I would not change our meeting and our love for one another. I presently am not going to. I have no intentions of ever-changing one second of our love together for the world. It is a God-given gift of grace.

This is the way I perceive things to be. I'm sure you will have a different perspective the other way, and that's what makes our relationship so exciting. I am so anxious, yet patiently, trudging through the happy road of destiny with my friend. And if we get called home and only have one friend, we are the lucky ones. We are blessed and very fortunate.

Looking back, these are experiences we learn from to some degree on some occasions. Some of those we need to block out of our memory forever and only God can do that. However, those bad experiences can be brought into someone else's life with ample light from heaven.

God can do for us what we cannot do for ourselves. I'm not sure how you read my emails to you when I send them to you consecutively all day long? I'm assuming, like most people, of course, you're not most people. We are one each and became two in friendship. And no matter how dark or grim things may appear to be, there is a silver lining on that cloud. And knowingly, we are not God and only acknowledge a tiny part of his love for us. You and I together have been able to tap into this love with the blessings coming through us from the Holy Spirit.

Let us do a little dreaming. Let us imagine that I certainly am getting this vasectomy reversal. I have worked hard to get this, and I only have you to thank for that. You are an angel sent to me from God above, with a lot of love. I'm going to talk a little sporadically, going back and forth, so do not get too confused.

Okay, I write as the thoughts come through me. And with you, my best friend in mind. The dreaming, I get the vasectomy reversal, a 60% chance to a 90% chance that it will be successful. Dr. could not determine that until after he gets into the operation. Because what determines that factor of percentages is how I originally had the vasectomy. At the time, Vasectomies were brand-new on the market.

Very few people had heard of them, and to find a doctor to perform them at the time, they had to be a doctor that was semi-teetering on the medical profession of being honest because they were against the law, so a friend of mine, God rest his soul since he was a bartender at a very exclusive restaurant.

I came across a doctor who was an alcoholic who said he would do it for my friend since my friend supplied him with liquor at the bar. And I remember he was an older gentleman, a little shaky with thick glasses, just the kind of guy you see in the movies. Smile, there are two ways of doing a vasectomy reversal. Dr. showed me on a piece of paper with the drawing of a penis and testicles. It was just a white piece of paper with a pencil outline, only one line of the penis and testicles, and Dr. proceeded to show me how he would have done this operation.

Since this first doctor was not legal, he did it the fast and dirty way. And that is good. That means he just cut the two sperm cords that come down and go into each testicle, on the outside of the testicle. I remember it was only like a 20-minute operation in the doctor's office, with no nurse available. So he put a tiny incision in the testicle, pulled the sperm tube through the incision, and proceeded to cut the tube and tie it off somehow.

Thomas wrote;

Beautiful, where was I? Was I about ready to lose that whole email? Through the incision, cut it, not sure how they tied off each end? Then put the cut tubes back in a couple of stitches in each testicle. An illegal but straightforward operation, what is the difference between 60% and 90%? And thank God for that operation that was sleazy, brought us up into the 90% range. On the other hand, I feel he did not go surgically because Dr. Heinz said they would have to go way inside my testicle to retie or reconnect the tubes. And I'm assuming it was not done that way. That looks too technical and needed a hospital.

With that being said, let's project our lives into the future as I was saying and interrupted by detail so you and I could both understand as I relive this experience. The future? We get married, God willing you get pregnant with our child, we live together, let us assume that it is here, or it could be anywhere else in this world, has not much to do with location.

Satan will be on us and after us, like you would not believe. I certainly hope you would pray, speak with your mother about, and think about it. And remember, I am a Marine. I can handle anything the devil has to throw at me because I know where he is coming from if it is negativity from other people. I feel I do not have to tell you what those trials and tribulations will consist of? You are too intelligent, and you are my girl.

My girl has to know that this Marine will stand behind his girl without a shadow of a doubt. Every step of the way and you can count on that. Because if I do not, for any reason, I can count on a trip to hell. I could speculate scenarios, but I feel you know what they are and who they will be coming from? Every jealous woman is barren or is not living the life that we are. Every man that sees me with a young woman that is so beautiful and pregnant with our child.

Other than your mother and God through Jesus Christ, our Lord's name went to the cross and died for a specific reason. So that others would have a place to go-to to forgive their sins that have transgressed against us. Please reread the above couple of sentences. Could you handle the humiliation? Could you take what you think people are saying about us?

I really cannot think of one person that would be happy for us. Believe it or not, there is one, and that one is Brian. Once again, you're right. He turned out to be a good friend. And there's nothing he would not do for either of us. You can take that to the bank. I witnessed him in action today with me, at the staff or medical facility hospital.

Thomas wrote;

Beautiful, I'm making up for lost time double smile I missed you, I do not want to lose this email to be a continued beautiful girl. Peace and grace of the Lord be with you, and your mother, through Jesus Christ of our Lord's name, amen.

I should get that small prayer in every email above. I pray to God you realize how much more I care for you. I know you already know? If that make sense? Like I have met you before, you are my guardian, you are my teacher, your strong spirit sent from above.

I will always show my love for this precious love that will continue into eternal life. With God the Father, Jesus Christ, his only Son our Lord, born of the Virgin Mary, Suffered under Pontius Pilate, was crucified, died, and was buried. On the third day, Jesus Christ, our Lord, arose from the dead, is now seated at the right hand of God the Father, waiting to judge the living and the dead. You and I believe in the communion of saints, the forgiveness of sins, and life everlasting. Amen,

You are my girl, and I told you lately that I missed you? I'm going to call you on your telephone right now and leave a message. Please try to remember this sentence and see if you can remember what message I left you. I might give you a hint, and then again, I may not, double trouble smile with the backflip just one backflip so far, stay tuned.

Just a footnote and a sporadic message, I could write a volume on the people that God placed in my life today. Uplifting their spirits and giving them something that they will think about.

I walked in this packed lobby of people, and I mean many people, standing room only maybe 100 people. The lady asked me behind the desk, can I please help you, sir. In a wheelchair, I seem to stand out as someone who needs help. Did she know I was a least there that need spiritual help for physical help? I'm right where God wants me at this very second. I said, "hallelujah, praise the Lord, thank you, Jesus, thank you, God, pass the blessings. In a Marine Corps command voice, with a big smile on my face, I mean everybody I was to observe was laughing.

I like to throw God in as often as I can in my humor that they will know spiritually that there is a God. A man in a wheelchair with one arm and happy as a clam at high tide. Letting as many souls know that this man finds communion with God. My positive way of looking at life and thinking that maybe there is a God, after all? This Marine knows something that others have not experienced, and he has been through hell. Possibly that's what they're thinking. That's what God tells me they are feeling.

And beautiful, how I acted or what I said spiritually would depend on your spiritual behavior if we were together. And this is only and if. If I were to act the way I acted today morally, and you were with me, how would you react? What do you think? I'm curious to know what my girl would think. I feel we should be proud to be in each other's presence, in front of that vast crowd of people. We could turn their lives around in a heartbeat. And there are so many out there that need our help spiritually, through the grace of God. Something money cannot buy——eternal life in heaven.

Now I'm saving the best part for last, and my mind went straight to the gutter. When I got home today, and left you a message. I went directly to bed without listening to my answering machine. When I woke up a few hours later and listened to the messages. I had two messages from the Dr., one stating that he would look forward to seeing me tomorrow for surgery.

The next one was from the Hospital administration said they were having a problem. With an insurance issue, two more messages from the hospital Dr. office letting me know that the surgery has been postponed and set for the original date. I will know tomorrow morning when I call them up on the telephone.

I called tonight and left a message with the nurse that was on duty and said she would most certainly get that message to Drs. Office, that I did get his message, and to not show up tomorrow. And keep in mind God can do for us what we cannot do for ourselves, and miracles do happen.

I will be on the telephone at 8 AM, finding out exactly why my surgery was canceled? And who canceled it? And what can I do to rectify this so-called problem? I reminded them that God did not feel it was a problem. A guardian angel sent me here to have this operation performed by God. So the surgery may well be completed tomorrow. If not, it is God's will, not mine.

I will pursue this with enthusiasm. And threaten them with the newspaper lawsuit if denied, that the United States military can pay three-quarters of $1 million for sex changes, and they cannot authorize a vasectomy reversal? That's how I got their attention in the first place. And I did not, God did, and the guardian angel, sent from God. And she is far more formidable and gracious, more so than this Marine, because she is my girl. And I will lay my life down for her, and God knows that, and God says this in the Bible, John 15; 13. that there is no greater love than this, that one should lay down his or her life for his friend or neighbor.

Another email looks like to be continued. You have some homework to do in between working and sleeping. See what you do when your friend misses you? Triple double backflip with a huge smile and big grinning face from ear to ear. We bring a lot of joy into each other's lives, would you not agree? Hugs and kisses to my friend from your friend, so take that to work, big triple, big double, big single big from the roof to the floor back up to the roof, smile.

Beautiful, you're not only a beautiful God-given gift from the outside, but you're even more beautiful on the inside. For that, I am proud of you. God is proud of us, and he loves us. Anyway, sweetheart, this is all speculation on my part, and I'm waiting for my girl to give me her feedback because your intuition far surpasses mine.

I was hoping you could share this with your mother as well. I would be interested in knowing her thoughts on the subject. And please let us all continuously pray that is all we have between the three of us is showing our love to God in Jesus Christ, his only begotten son, through our prayers.

Acknowledge our love for God and Jesus Christ, letting a Holy Spirit work through us to help others. A little indicator was my Dr., you remember her? She is the jealous Dr. said, "does the rest of your family know about this crazy idea" that told me volumes. And she is a doctor from the medical profession? Give me a break. Romans 14; 10. But why do you judge thy brother? Or why do you not judge your brother? For we shall all stand before the judgment seat of Christ.

Satan is alive and well. And good old Dr. Heinz could hardly wait to spread the rumor throughout the medical profession and community. Tells you where his mind is at? Take what I have said into consideration, realizing and understand that we could come together beautifully, and for some unknown reason, could be short-lived.

It is not through our own, but a sacrifice to the world that they have destroyed and damaged two beautiful children of God that they know they should not have. And we will have to pay the price for their sins. Now, are you willing to go there? And this is not speculation. I have observed these things so far, and the cat is not even out of the bag yet. I will stand by you every inch of the way, and I will fight and kill, and Satan knows that. Others can only trample on us unless it is in a very devious way.

We love this one. I'm sending this off now, beautiful, because you're my girl, and I do not send these emails to make you sad only for the reality of you.

Together we both know what could more likely happen. You are my precious angel and my girl, and I thank God for you and your mother. Please make sure your mother knows that my prayers are with her until the next email, to be continued.

Well I left you a telephone message, and I'm getting tired, so I don't know when I'm going to go to bed. My eyeballs are telling me, in my mind and my heart, and the consumption of you. Revitalize and revises and pumps air back into the spirit about ready to go to sleep, unsure if I will, not sure if I can, only God knows.

This is my friend God, and I pray that through Jesus Christ our Lord and dying for our sins, you please take care of my friend DiAnnie and her mother Anna, bringing joy into their lives. In a way that they will know that my love for you, and everything written in your word concerning the Bible. I know my faith and prayers that God will protect and provide for DiAnnie and her mother in a way that I cannot at present.

Spiritually you know, God our Father, that we store our riches in heaven, not of this earth. Where rust and moths can deteriorate them, this is an eternal love that you have for us, and we have for you. Through your son Jesus Christ our Lord's name this we pray this day amen.

Matthew 6; 19. Lay not up to yourselves treasures upon earth, where moth and rust do corrupt, and where thieves break through and steal.

And I also pray to God that the delay in surgery was not out of someone's human jealousy. I can imagine, and I know I should not think of these things, but understanding that

I am not perfect and only my girl can provide excellent knowledge. I could flip a coin whether this was God's will or Satan trying to interfere.

This saga will be continued because Satan knows, and he knows, that I know, I quit dancing with him a long time ago, and he knows me. I know him, but he loves to come after me from time to time. Although the devil forgets, he even tempted Jesus in the garden of Gethsemane and continuously harass Jesus throughout his ministry. And finally nailed Him to the cross, thinking of course that he had gotten his way.

You see, the devil is not that intelligent, he knows scripture very well, but he likes to twist it and turned around, so you think it's your fault.

And I have danced with the devil, I trip to the light fantastic, I did a little soft shoe, and then I did the Boogaloo, spun him around and bid him farewell, and never look back, Jack.

I feel the devil likes me to slam dunk him from time to time to make him angry enough, "angry," that word angry? To keep coming after me because he loves pain. No one can give him more pain than Jesus Christ the Lord and God the father. The Holy Spirit is working through me with the knowledge and wisdom of God through his word.

The evil spirits know Jesus Christ's name. They see the apostle Paul's name, and they know my name. Unshakable faith knows this to be accurate, that I will always care for you no matter what the devil has to send his little helpers at me, and there are thousands of them, literally thousands.

Beautiful girl, sweet dreams, I pray you to have sweet dreams this I pray for that they are a sweet, kind, generous, and happy joyous, with love consideration of my girl's character. Peace, and enjoy with prayers and all the good things that heaven has to offer. This I pray, that my girl has dreams of pleasant sweet things, that are meant to be enjoyed.

Do you realize how much I missed you? You have no idea, do you? Are you even concerned? Here comes the other me, and here I am to teach myself about me, because of you, beautiful. Now that was not a good thing to say. Go back and erase that. She does not need to read that?, Yes you dumbhead, nobody says those negative things to anybody, only you, Thomas, from time to time going off in your head, well I don't know what to say or what to do?

Your brain is fried, Thomas. Do you see why I cry?, No you ignoramus, what did you say to me? I did not understand the word? Figures; ignoramus means bright shining ignorance. Now, does that make sense? How can your ignorance be bright and shiny? Get over it, get to bed before I beat you with the belt, tie you up for two weeks, and switch you continuously. Did you understand that my little kid needs a good whipping? Did you ask me finally to go to bed?

Be sweet to you until your heart melts, fly me to heaven for two weeks, sweet kisses continuously? All I can say, Thomas, you need prayer and a lot of it. Although I will, from time to time, continually educate you. Of your character defects, intelligence with respect, love, safe faith, we have a long ways to go through, you're not even close? I did not say, and I told you you could count on it. Here's the baseball bat to watermelon head, Thomas.

I could not help myself. I had to talk to myself before I go to sleep, which calms my nerves. I should quit talking to myself like that, and I have to have some fun. I might as well be talking to myself, and I could be saying this to other people, a smile.

Does my double mind talk amuse you? Or can it make you sad? I ask you this seriously out of consideration, care for you and your feelings. With love and kindness, no disrespect intended or to hurt or make you sad. I have hurt you enough over the last past year. I fully intend not to anymore. I could erase these things above before emailing them. I really should.

From now on, I'm going to keep it positive in a fun way. The above was the last. I pray to God that you will get to read any negativity from me. You are my angel, you are my teacher, you are my guide to heaven, and together, we can go to heaven when God calls us home. Not one moment before or one moment after, God will come like a thief in the night. We know not when.

Let your mother know that you and she are both in my prayers, and please pray for me hard. I feel that's how we got together initially. God already knew the answer to our prayers before asking, only when all three of us asked. That's when the miracle happened. For that, I cannot thank God enough for you in my life. I care, hugs and kisses.

God had seen that you had suffered enough, and he says enough. A blessing is coming to you. Believing in God, today and tomorrow are going to be the days of your life. I'm learning thanks to you.

Ephesians 4; 29 - don't use foul or abusive language, even thoughts in your mind. Everything you say or think be excellent and helpful so that words will encourage those who hear them. That does it—no more conversations with myself. I am my own worst enemy in my head, left to my own devices. I am in trouble.

Proverbs 21; 23 - whoever keeps his mouth and his tongue keeps himself out of trouble.

I must work on this one, especially with my mind and my stinking thinking. Realizing that's what I adore is your intuitive spiritual wisdom, wait on the Lord, and he will avenge you.

In my mind's eye, I find that you have the patience that is beyond my understanding. But I know it through prayer was sent from God above, with a lot of love. And you have shown me a lot of love. You not only tell me about your pet but show me in a way that I can understand.

And I think to myself, God, this angel is precious and should have dumped me a long time ago. I find her instructing me with patience that only a beautiful lady with this Marine, that God knew would bring him to his knees. You do things that are honorable in such a way that everyone can see you as reliable.

Galatians 5; 19 - 20 - - - the acts of the flesh are evident; love immorality, impurity, and debauchery; idolatry and witchcraft; hatred, discord, jealousy, fits of rage, selfish ambitions, dissensions, factions, and envy; drunkenness, orgies, and the like. As I did before, I warn you that those who live like this will not inherit the kingdom of God. Psalms 85; 10 - - love and faithfulness meet together, righteousness and peace kiss each other.

Beautiful, when I tell you this, if I have my life to live again, next time, I would find you sooner so I could love you longer. When we love one another and grow in love stronger with the bond lasting longer into an eternity with God, neither of us will understand.

Psalms 139 - you are fearfully and wonderfully made.

This is my one-liner from God to me to you, you are fearfully made, that you hook up with the United States Marine Corps Sgt., and you show no fear because you wonderfully made, I am putty in your hands, in a moment God is crying with you, because you are wonderfully made.

A God-given gift of grace. I thank God for you, not only yourself but your mother as well. Of whom has played a significant part in this bond of a family we have created through God. Do you not agree? This is how I feel, and I care for you with hugs and kisses your my girl.

I heard this on a ministry show I was listening to. I do not understand my wife. She does not make me happy. Maybe it's because you haven't had a fresh idea in six years. Do not criticize your wife or point out her faults. It was those same faults that kept her from getting a better husband. As a result, the audience laughed - and the preacher said, "and all the ladies said," and all 5000 of the ladies in the audience shouted, "AMEN."

Satan is the father of lies and appears to be the great light. As he told Eve in the Garden of Eden, you do not need God. You can be as good as God. You do not need to obey God, and she took the bite of the forbidden fruit gave to her husband, Adam. When God is asking questions, God is not looking for answers. God asked Adam, why did you do that? Adam said she did it, she is the one who gave it to me, and God asked Eve why did you eat the forbidden fruit, and she said, because you put the snake in the garden who tempted me, you did it.

And God sent the two angels with flaming swords to Drive them out into this world we live in today. For the remembrance of our sins from the garden of Eden up until this current date. Women shall know the pain of bearing children, and men shall toil with the weeds and thistles the rest of Their lives.

God will only give us what we can handle and no more. Beautiful, think about what I have to endure, the cross that I carry. This may be the age difference factor. You would have to be one tough lady to help maintain the cross or even want to. Isn't life hard enough with all the extracurricular activities? Nothing happens perchance in God's world. Everything happens for a reason. And we came together for a perfect explanation, we teach each other, and we will continue throughout the rest of our lives.

You can say few words, and I can write volumes. Please think about everything that I have written to you in the last several hours. I do not send any of these words to hurt you or make you feel sad, or break your heart. I dream about us being together one day for eternity. God has promised me that would be true.

19 October 2018

Thomas wrote;

Beautiful peace and grace be with you and your mother through Jesus Christ our Lord amen

I feel I must start with some prayer because God loves his children that show a lot of love for God. Between you and I would be great. Sometimes, the least words said to have the most impact on meaning.

You are my consumption of thought and feelings, and I look forward to your comments that are so precious to my soul. They are my journey to heaven. Have a good day, sweetheart. Take care of yourself, be nice to yourself, and try to make the people around you happy. You are lifting their trials and tribulations from others, although they still have a cross to carry. And the trials and tribulations you go to or witness will find out the precious soul you are giving as a person in need. This world is of Satan, the whole world that was offered to Jesus Christ, as Satan took Jesus up to the top of the Temple Mount and showed him the world as a whole. Jesus said, "get behind me, Satan, and do not tempt God your creator.

You are my girl. I care about you and think about you. Your words have many meanings. This I know. You are my angel, precious soul that has been brought into my life. I lived my whole life to finally meet you get together with my angel, my guardian angel. Your beautiful hugs and kisses

Possibly a couple of suggestions. I'm just going to throw them out there, too, I am projecting. Only God knows for sure the answer to our prayers, of what we need. What is right for us is things we do not know. Possibly for some reason, I couldn't have children with you, because of the unsuccessful operation, we could adopt babies. There are many in this world. People would most certainly have a different outlook and perspective of us getting together.

You bring a friend with you, stay for a while, and then fly back to The North Country with your friend. And stay in the master bedroom, and you will have access to the master bathroom, with a Jacuzzi and a steam shower. We come together as good friends. I would enjoy lying in bed with you and holding, no kissing. I have read too many psychological failures 1000% for sure that it inevitably leads to intercourse when you start kissing. And I strongly feel that we must be married if we are going to go there.

There is nothing more intriguing or enticing than a love novel for the soul.

Keep in mind that the story in the back chapter? It is about a love between you and me, and God blesses us. We could raise our family and help others get to the gates of heaven. Our family consists of your mother and the two of us, which makes three of us. You are my girl, and I care for your hugs and kiss, be of good cheer says, Jesus.

Thomas wrote;

Beautiful, Don't waste time on what's not essential. Do not get sucked into the drama. Get on with it; don't dwell on the past.; be generous of spirit, the person you admire. In doing so, you will draw real friends, and as I have mentioned before, if we get called home and only have one, we are very fortunate.

I know, and I feel in my heart that you are my friend, and there's nothing we would not do for each other. I would give my life for you in a heartbeat without looking back and without any type of regrets or resentments because you are my girl.

Galatians 5; 15 - 16 -However, if you continually bite and devour one another, but I say, live in the spirit, and you will not carry out the desires of the flesh.

Corinthians 3; 3 – For ye are yet carnal; for whereas there is among you envying, and strife, and divisions, are you not carnal, and walk as men?

This has nothing to do with you, just your own business.—1 Theologians 4; 11. Also, make it your goal to live quietly, do your work, and earn your living, as we ordered you.

You have a good day, sweetheart. Take care of yourself: beautiful hugs and kisses, your friend and my girl.

Thomas wrote;

Have a great day, be nice to yourself, do not take any wooden nickels, smile, do not do anything I would not do, and if you do, do not name it after me, triple smile with the big ski jump. As soon as I find out what's going on with my surgery, I will keep you updated. You might call me tomorrow morning in a storm, where we may or may not be able to say hi to each other. And I will expect possibly an email from my northern treasure, either Monday night or Tuesday morning. Beautiful, do not work too hard and get some rest. You're my girl.

Peace and grace with joy and happiness with God our Lord be with you and your mother through Jesus Christ our Lord name amen.

Thomas wrote;

Beautiful, how is your mother doing? Where is she at? And how is life treating her? And is she happy? Just out of curiosity, none of my business, but you mentioned to me that you did not like the friend or guy she was living with. I feel there was a perfect reason. I do not want to hear things like that, you know me; I despise men who mistreat, take advantage, use or treat ladies like slaves, thinking ladies are lesser than thou, or abuse ladies, making me sick. It's just who I am. I consider ladies to be angels, just above men, as God considers angels just above creation.

The hospital calls me right now and said that there was a problem with scheduling. Since I am flexible and know that I let them know, they apologized profusely and couldn't be more subservient and appreciative, and I also let them know how grateful I was and to please let my Dr. Heinz know that my prayers are with him and thank him.

If something is hard and you could make a difference in someone's life, take the easy route instead of your own. I'm not sure from explaining myself correctly. If things are hard and your force your way through them, I suggest turnaround and go downhill. That's not right. If you can make someone else's life easier, by all means, do it. How's that? To simplify my mind,

I appreciate you, my girl DiAnnie, you are a great friend, and I enjoy immensely talking to you or writing to you. I would say putting my mouth on you by talking. Triple, quadruple smile with the triple forward backflip, with the double twist, a jackknife, and back in my chair. Don't ask me to do that again, smile small smile but smiling.

One thing I wanted to write back and forth about, and I pray to God you do not take this the wrong way or think I'm trying to control you. It's just that we should talk about things that could happen in the future between the two of us, and very well may not. Then try not to take them seriously, just something to think about only in case. And there's nothing wrong with dreaming about being on the dream team. Is there?

I have such a big heart, and I care for children equally with ladies, both of them can bring me to my knees. Make me cry, or turn me into a "Tough Marine" if anyone harmed a small child or a lady. I pray you can understand that.

As I have mentioned above, we would have to discuss this between us because of your intuition, intelligence, wisdom, knowledge, a beautiful young lady, of course, my girl, I'm like a child waiting for a candy bar. A smile I'm not sure if it would be a good idea to expose our children to the way people would treat them or us, that would come from satan.

And I know you know what I'm talking about. It would turn me into one Marine. My reputation around here perceives me. I cannot think of one person that I am fearful of except for God. And everyone knows that who knows me, and I get a lot of respect because of that. That's just who I am.

Others know who I am and what I am capable of doing. I feel in that respect. God may have me here for a reason. Kind of like, has a reputation. People have told me that they saw somebody and they mention my name, and they say I know him when they don't.

On occasion, someone will tell a story from my past. One thing I have never done is changed in that respect, other than gain a lot of spiritual discernment through the Bible and quite a few more miracles. I never doubted God's existence ever since I was a little tiny kid When I was Zorro. Smile from you and a smile for me.

You realize, of course, I am reading in this far more than what it is. Don't you just love my imagination? Do not say the word, and I'll say it no, a big no, with a big sad face no.

And please do not get frustrated with all my emails, and the best thing you could do, more than likely, is to flash through them. And to say, I read all your emails, big double, triple smile quadruple backflip bumped my head on the ceiling, placed my head back on the floor bounce over into the chair here, I am.

I care for you to think about you. What do you think about that speculation?

It is called journaling. It's like pouring your heart out to the one you care about, like becoming best friends and strengthening that friendship with the spot of superglue. What I'm saying is just dumb through the emails, and keep in mind that I am journaling; one thing writers always regret from what I have read is that they never journaled daily. As a result, the writers that have journaled daily are renowned and moviemakers. These journals may not appear to anyone at any time, but they do submerge later down the road. They will be worth a blessing that God would have two give to someone with some insight.

You're my girl. Make sure and tell your mother my prayers are with her, and like I have mentioned the questions above, I know your mother spiritually is a compelling woman with God. When she told you to tell me, "respect him," you recall that conversation. No mother tells her daughter that or mentions that to her daughter without a spiritual connection with God. I have never even heard of a mother saying something like that to her daughter when the mother has not even met this gentleman the daughter is talking about.

And I believe you're getting to know me a little bit, just a drop in the bucket better, possibly. What I feel foolish about, and I still think about it, you know one of those moments you are embarrassed to even think about? When speaking on the telephone with your mother for the first time, not realizing that she could not speak one English word. It did not show respect. You can please ask your mother if she can forgive me. You may have forgotten that. I'm not sure your mother did. I know I haven't.

Have a good day, beautiful. My prayers are with you. You and your mother say prayers for me, and I will say prayers for both of you with care.

Thomas wrote;.

Isn't this attractive beautiful? I'm working just as hard as you are, a small smile debatable smile. I work so hard physically all my life until the time I could not, and guess what? There will come a time in everyone's life if we are fortunate to live to a ripe old age, that we will no longer be able to work. And I let everyone know, work as long as you can, as often as you can, there will come a time when you will not be able to work.

Fortunately, or unfortunately, God has me right where I need to be, and I accept that. Just some interesting facts that I ran across that I thought you might be interested in. Scheduled surgery. They do not know what time as of yet. I did mention to you that the way they will have to determine whether this operation was successful. According to the nurse practitioner, a female, I did not get into any conversation with her. She said to me, and you could either try it out on your wife or take a sperm sample. I said, how are you going to do that?

She said, "can you bring us a sample?" I will ask her or the doctor, if I were to collect a sperm sample, how would I transport to the hospital? And where would I bring it too? And how long can the sperm remain before it is not testable?

And I would certainly like to thank you again. I appreciate my guardian angel getting my soul to heaven, even for some reason, we do not follow through with our relationship as husband and wife here on this earth. In the spiritual aspect, when I get to heaven, God will not ask me the question.

My computer is messing up badly, I'm going to lay down and dream about us, and I pray I have a good dream because you are my girl.

Thomas wrote;

And I care no pressure. Have you felt any pressure from anything I have said? Those are not my intentions, never will be your happiness and well-being, and your mother is my intentions and care and prayers.

Thomas wrote;

Brian has to keep busy looking for my driver's license. Now we know where it is not. It is not in my car. Next, we are moving to the shower. It could be under the film inside the shower. We will move throughout the house looking for the driver's license. I keep myself busy mentally.

I worked out about an hour ago in a continuously fast and pray. And I will work out again tonight, and I will study and read the Bible. It takes some viable tests. Some of that scripture that I sent you did not pertain to you or me, so please do not take it personally.

Brian brought a friend over, I thought it was a male, and he asked me if he could bring her in to introduce her to me, and I said, it is a female? You're going to start paying rent right now, I told you no females, and we made a deal that you're going to start paying the thousand dollars a month if you decide to have a female life with you in your little shack. Big smile, more giant smile thinking about it. When I meet his friend I'm going to ask her if she would buy us dinner tonight? Triple, triple, quadruple smile, Brian and her are going shopping, very little, the least she could do is buy us dinner.

Do we disagree? I will keep this email open until after I meet her. Brian said he had to put her makeup on blah blah blah double bluff plan blah blah blah not the bluff plan. I pray I have a good dream because you are my girl.

Thomas wrote;

Peace, and grace with the Lord be with you and your mother through Jesus Christ our Lord's name amen,

Our Father who art in heaven, hallowed be the name, thy kingdom come thy will be done, on this earth as it is in heaven, give us this day our daily bread and forgive us our trespasses, as we forgive those who trespass against us, and lead us not into temptation, but deliver us from evil, for thine is the kingdom the power and the glory forever amen. (Notice that heaven is mentioned twice in this prayer by Jesus)

God, grant me the serenity to accept the things I cannot change, the courage to change the things I can, and the wisdom to know the difference.

Thomas and DiAnnie believe in one God, the Father Almighty, Creator of heaven and earth. In Jesus Christ, his only son, our Lord, born of the Virgin Mary, suffered under Pontius Pilate, was crucified, died, and was buried. On the third day, Jesus rose from the dead, ascended into heaven, and is now seated at the right hand of God the Father, waiting to judge the living and the dead. Thomas and DiAnnie believe in saints' communion, the forgiveness of sins, and life everlasting amen.

Hail Mary, full of grace the Lord is with thee, blessed art thou amongst women and blessed is the fruit of thy womb Jesus, Holy Mary mother of God pray for us sinners now. At the hour of our death, amen.

I attended parochial school in the first and second grades. It was rigorous back then; Regiment and military in nature and sisters taught us, long white John. With the habit on their head with the black veil that came down the back. And they were mean. You think I'm tough. I learned the contrition act above, the apostle's Creed above, the Hail Mary above, with the wooden ruler across the knuckles.

When the bell rang, there were two lines in front of the classroom, the boys on one line and the girls. We all had to wear uniforms, great salt-and-pepper pants, a dark gray long-sleeved shirt, and a maroon sweater. The girls had to wear blue plaid skirts that were below their knees, a white blouse with a maroon sweater, and they had to wear sandals, not sandals. I forget what those shoes are cold that girl seems to wear back then, black-and-white or brown and white tied up the front to the ankles. And if we got caught chewing bubblegum or gum, we had to stick the gum on our nose and put our head in the corner.

The girl's discipline was to put their nose in the corner of the room against the wall. The boys got whacked across the knuckles with a ruler. I got caught jaywalking one day by 1/3 grader, and I was in the first grade, he took me up to Mother Superior's office, she was about 4 foot nothing, she said to lift your shirt in the office in front of about ten people, now bend over she said. I swear her feet came off the ground, three wax across the back with approximately an 18-inch garden hose.

She then said, now we are not going to do that anymore, or we? No sister superior, and we had to go to church every morning. And if the sisters asked us what color the Catholic priest was wearing and we did not know that we did not go to mass. We always did not go to mass. This is the reason. Catholic kids are so mean, is we go to confession on Fridays to help our sins to a Catholic father, which meant to us, that we could sin the rest of the week. Because we knew next Friday, we were going to clean the chalkboard of our soul again.

The Our Father came from Jesus Sermon on the Mount, "Matthew 6; 9 - 14, Jesus sermon on the Mount was from the chapters of Matthew 5,6 and 7. Jesus starts the sermon on the Mount with the nine Beatitudes.

I have all of these prayers memorize, and believe it or not. I say them daily from time to time helps keep me focused and relaxed meditate in prayer. I know it might sound structured, but it works for me, and I do talk to God one on one as I'm sure you will know by now. Hugs and kisses, have a good day get some rest, and when you feel rested at your convenience, if you feel like it, if the spirit moves, you either write me or call me. Remember, at your convenience, do not force yourself or feel obligated to, okay? Hugs and kisses

Thomas wrote;

Brian's girlfriend Cindy, I had to mention that I do not commit adultery, and I do not fornicate, so do not get any wise ideas. Because she came right in and threw her arms around me, giving a great big hug, I said, do not think you are going to park your body in my bed anytime soon, big triple-double smile.

Hence, she and Brian went to pick up a few groceries and Chinese dinner for all three of us. Of course, I am a gentleman and know that will be a short visit she brought her car. Thank God she said she was raised with six children. Her father was a trucker. She had one of those operations where they remove a lady's breast. She had to tell me that for whatever reason.

It took her one hour to get her makeup on. She has a real outgoing personality. I always look forward to meeting new people. I would never meet with the lady one on one other than it being just business or needing directions. I do not invite strange ladies into my house. I usually greet them at the front door and talk on the front porch.

Because I have a girl, and even before we had met, this is who I am and not interested in ladies. I devote my life to God and service, then I wrote my prophecy and thinking about and praying about a soulmate that I had imagined was in heaven. I almost knew in my spirit and my mind that she was in heaven waiting for me. Then, my girl, beautiful DiAnnie, tapped me on the shoulder. I turned around, and there you were. And you know what happened after that? I question God in a state of shock and disbelief.

And here we are, sweetheart, my beautiful girl. I will write you more later, about my visit with Brian and Cindy. I'm going to lay down and get some rest. I'm going to need it for her stay. Otherwise, I will get a migraine headache. She is one of these women who never shut up. Of course, I have great respect for ladies and offer her friendship, courtesy, and consideration.

Because that's who I am, as long as she is with another man and a friend of mine, Brian, everything is okay. And Brian is happy that she met me because evidently, he never shuts up about me.

One positive thing about not get the surgery today is that it will allow me to get my driver's license Monday. And an opportunity to finish my media profile for the publisher. I sent them an email yesterday and said that I was going in for an operation and would not have time to finish it. They sent me an email back totally understanding and asked me to get to them as soon as possible when I feel like it, and they said they hope everything went well with my operation.

At the time, neither of us knew it was going to be postponed. I will be working the weekend on that, anyway, beautiful just to keep you up with the juicy gossip and as the world squirms. You take care of yourself, do not work so hard, and I know you will work hard trying to have fun doing it and enlighten the customers to take their minds off the trials and tribulations, and that I also know you do because you're my girl. Hugs and kisses. Beautiful sweet DiAnnie, I care for you more than you think whether I say some things that may not let you think so, and I apologize for those words. You are my teacher.

DiAnnie wrote;

So does not think old Cindy is going on a shopping spree anytime soon hugs and kisses.

My sweet girl DiAnnie - you must feel safe, protected, cared for, and know in yours. heart of hearts that out of 7 billion people, there is just one that cares

Thomas wrote;

Beautiful, I would like you to. Know how much you can depend on me and that I will never belittle you in front of anyone, I would die for you, and I will stick up for you; I will protect you and care for you. You must feel safe secure and that you can trust me with honesty and telling you everything.

Through God, I would know how to treat you with the tremendous respect and the love of a holy soul that has been sent with heavenly grace to my life because you are my girl.

You are precious not only in the eyes of God mine as well. As well as your mother, so please do not feel intimidated or shy, or insecure. Feel confident that you have a great understanding and a voice that will draw many people to you. Who will want to be around you to know who you are and what kind of precious lady you are? Because you are my girl,

Brian and Cindy are still not back. I pray to God that woman does not spend any or not one penny more than what I asked Brian to pay.

Because she is Brian's friend, and that's who I am, and this is what the spirits tell me. I have done this all my life is to give it all away to keep it. And I believe you mentioned the word selfish to me at one point time, which made me sad and sick to my stomach. This was quite a while back. I just know the feeling, and it was just the process of getting acquainted with one another, nothing other than that. Nothing will ever be repeated, and I do not keep trying to revive a dead horse.

Once something is said that is not right, you have taught me a lesson, and I will thank you for that, and I will always thank you for that. And this is how our love for one another will grow into a passion that neither of us has experienced. That each of us has dreamed about, and God can do for us what we cannot do for ourselves. So expect miracles when we are together you will witness them and give thanks and praise to God for them.

Because we both know the love that God has for both of us and your mother because you are my girl, so feel safe know that you can trust me no matter what you do or what you say, everything is okay. And I would be there every step of the way with you, to grow in this unknown love that we have not fully yet experienced. However, we are still making the cake and making a great cake, only the kind that God would have us make. And has to be right before we can even think of taking a bite.

A small smile, you're my girl. I would imagine sending you another email or two just to let you know how the evening is going or went. Because I care hugs and kisses

I recall that the nurse practitioner said that when I questioned her at Dr. Heinz's office, she said it would be 3 to 6 months. I'm not sure I quite understood what she was speaking of at the time. Another question I will have. How long will it take for the cycle of Sperm to be productive and why? It seemed to me they do not explain in detail too much about the questions I have for them that I feel they should know and would have offered to let me know. One day at a time, everything is okay right now. Everything is okay, A-okay.

You take care of yourself be nice to yourself. I cannot repeat this enough to get plenty of rest because I care about the number of friends who care, sincerely care, something you do not realize or understand possibly. I'm sure more than likely that I am your friend. After a time, I pray to God that I am your only friend, and I would give my life for you with no hesitation.

I heard a story the other day, a gentleman walked into a cancer ward to visit, and there was a little boy with his father, the visitor noticed the little boy with the band on his head, and his father was tall 6 foot two inches, real dark wavy hair, real handsome gentleman. This other man came back a week or two later. He was surprised, the tall good looking gentleman had shaved his head bald, and the little boy comes running over to this gentleman who was visiting the cancer ward, see my dad shaved his head just like me, and now we are going to let our hair grow out together. That's love. Peace and grace be with you and your mother through Jesus Christ our Lord's name amen.

20 October 2018

Thomas wrote;

Beautiful, Put some thought into this talk it over with your mother, please, and let me know how to move forward with our lives. And I'm not saying this to put pressure on you. That's the last thing I would want to do. I care about you, and you are my guardian angel and my girl, and I do not wish to hurt you or make you sad. I want you to be happy. All I want in life is to make you glad you have made me happy. God has made me happy by bringing you into my life.

And to not appreciate a God-given gift, the gift of grace means I will not be going to heaven. I have time we do not know for whatever that is worth. Please do not take it personally; the time here on this earth is short, and I'm not considering my lifetime.

I'm assuming the time before Jesus Christ will come in the clouds and take those souls to heaven with him that are deserving.

A God-given feeling is that through this book, there is an opportunity to save many souls and waiting patiently. Unfortunately, it is not an option to God, or the purpose for us being here and come together with the way that we have. has only brought this love of life. And a God-given thought not to mine you are my girl I am your Zorro, hugs, and kisses.

Thomas wrote;

I spend a lot to send books to prisons and give them to people I feel would help. And I believe I have mentioned to you how I signed my books, "Thomas inspired to write this book with spiritual discernment to help others, not for profit or prestige, proceeds donated." A love so special between you and Me that could only come from God would not defile that love. It is precious in my eyes.

My faith is unshakable. I am aware that if I want or would like my girl in my life and have children together with her. God knows this is not for fun. I know this. It is not fun if I cannot provide for my wife and my children, the very fortunate thing about us meeting and communicating online is that having the opportunity and the incentive to make a lot. Providing for my family is my goal and would be the answer to my dream and prayer. God knows this before I do because he knew of you and me before we did.

Although you read chapter 47 of my second book, you can read my prophecy before I even met you. And that came from God, and God put you in my life at that time. This is only a miracle of the biblical proportion of many I have experienced throughout my life. This is the message of a love that only God could give us that no one has ever experienced because they do not walk in our shoes and guide lost souls.

Now keep this in mind. This will take some time. I am a man who cares about this lady and her mother. I am not into disappointing ladies, especially when it comes to taking care of them. We will stay patiently communicating online this way until I can take care of you, our family, and your mother.

I have so much faith and love for God in Jesus Christ, our Lord. I continuously think about them. I read about the mind of God and what he wants for us. And it is not poverty. Do you believe God put us together to watch a starve to death and let Satan have his way? I don't think so, and now with that being said, I do not write for fun.

I am talking about an autobiography, nonfiction, real-life events from the time I was born; now that might be fun for some people. I always have given everything away to keep it, and I mean always, and God knows this. And I have been blessed beyond measure spiritually, and it was God that blessed me. I worked physically really hard and was able to provide.

It is because I spent quite a bit on drugs, alcohol, gambling. I cannot tell you that I will provide for you; only God knows that. This is why I say for you and your mother to pray and pray specifically for our needs. If you're praying to the moon or just for fun, God is not going to hear our prayers.

Here is our prayer together, okay, as God's children, Anna DiAnnie and Thomas, through the grace and peace of our Lord, and in Jesus Christ our Lord's word, that God can provide some security in these lady's lives.

I asked this with the faith and the miracles that I have been shown throughout life. God hears our prayer. You know God that with those blessings, we will help thousands of other people and bring them into your light, and God willing, we will be able to guide souls here on this God-given earth that Satan now controls.

Oh, Jesus Christ, our Lord hears our prayers. You are so precious in our eyes. We understand these prayers will not be answered if even one of us is being deceitful or dishonest.

And we do not know our souls and that we will be selfish and not help other people. We understand these prayers will not be answered. Jesus will say, go, I never knew you.

Even though we have said, we have done things of Jesus Christ in our Lord's name and did everything that Jesus asked us to do, but there was a black spot for our selfish selves in our hearts.

And for that reason, our prayers will not be answered. We pray this through Jesus Christ our Lord's name that Anna DiAnnie and Thomas prayers are heard because our hearts are pure and our intentions are good. We cannot walk on water. We cannot part the Red Sea. We will continuously need your help Jesus and guidance from the Holy Spirit that we do the right thing, as we will continually pray and give you thanks through Jesus Christ our Lord's precious name this we pray amen.

My girl DiAnnie, please pass this prayer onto your mother, and if you can both see it together over the telephone or say this to your mother. She can concentrate on the prayer. Any two or more are gathered in Jesus Christ our Lord's name.

Matthew 18; 20. For where two or three are gathered together in my name, there am I in the midst of them. It shall be done. Only in honesty and truth and faith can this prayer be answered. The girl that God brought into my life to show me God's love, hugs, and kisses.

Thomas wrote;

Beautiful, I have a feeling you will be tying me up all the time, aren't you? I will not enjoy it, but I will be laughing so hard it would be effortless for you to tie me up. As soon you pull out the rope, I will be laughing till I fall on the ground. I will make it easy for you.

Cindy told me that Brian was going to die pretty soon. From what I do not know. Unfortunately, he has grown on me and has a good heart, he cannot push me in my wheelchair over 50 feet without having to sit down, and I tell him, do not die on me here, Brian, wait till you get me to where I'm supposed to be going and then die.

At the time, I did. not realize how serious it is until Cindy told me. And he is in the perfect place to get called home and with a child of God to guide into the Christian transition and then, God willing, to heaven. Correcting him every time he damns God, but he does not do it anymore. Every time someone says that it hurts my heart, Cindy said it twice.

Those who created the pain of the present do not control the pleasure of the future.

I busted her, and they always tell me their sorry I said, do not tell me your sorry, ask God for forgiveness.

Anyway, how we perceive things to be and how they are, entirely two different things. That's what makes life so exciting, and only God can see through the trials and tribulations and the invisible things not seen. It merely mystifies the mind; God's love is vast and numerous compared to the things that are seen. And so many are unaware or blind.

Ladies love romance, and men are always intrigued when they get into the lady's pants. As the old saying goes, "love sells," and God has nothing against making love, or none of us would be here right now.

If you're not faithful and believing the numbers only, you might find another man because I have nothing to offer right now. And I may not for some time. You have to be more than a real girl; you have to be a girl with faith with works and turn your life over to the care of God, 100%. If you hold back 1% from God, I'm afraid the prayers will not be answered, and God knows your heart; He knows the number of hairs on your head. And we are just a small grain of sand on the beach.

You will always be my girl, like I have mentioned prior in the previous email. You are my girl and have shown me love that only God has to offer us and that beautiful is free for the asking and the taking. Hugs and kisses.

I do not write for fun; if I were going to write for fun, I would be writing to many people to have fun with them. I do not do that.

Thomas wrote;

Beautiful, I have had a little experience with the ladies, and I could be wrong. Cindy is looking for a trailer or a place to live. She has a brother in Los Angeles who has contacts with moviemakers who tell me Brian is dying. We are all going to die. We are not going to heaven until we die now if Brian does let Cindy move in with him, in that small shack of a guesthouse.

I feel she will make a move on me, and of course, I will throw her out of here instantly. What do you think? She came into the house by herself and said a few things that I felt were not appropriate. Like wiggling her butt in front of me, stretching high in my closet with her pants falling, saying she needs a belt. I turn my head instantly, thinking maybe it was just coincidental.

I know what to do; I do not want her moving here, especially into Brian's house. I told Brian if you choose to live with a woman in that shack, you're going to start paying rent. I'm sticking to that, and I feel Cindy has alternative motives. I could be wrong; I could be miss perceiving; this is why I need your feedback; what do you think once again?

You are my girl, and you're my friend; you are the love that God put into our lives together. We have spent a lot of time together. I do not write for fun. I write to you with compassion with care, with love, and I'm learning consideration for your feelings, emotions, and intuition. Run this by your mother. She may have some intuitive ideas, with a big smile and a big smile, knowing you are reading this, hugs and kisses.

Peace and Grace from the Lord our Father be with you and your mother through Jesus Christ our Lord's name amen.

Your mother is a gracious lady in my life, and she is a lady who has a daughter I care about. And the reason I care for this daughter is she is a God-sent and a miracle. And therefore, I honor and respect her mother, and I humble myself before her through the grace of God because she is the matriarch and one of God's elect.

This I feel spiritual, your mother has a lot of knowledge and wisdom and a lot to teach others. And she is your mother that I can show respect for and appreciate and let her know as a mother that my mother is no longer with us. She was called home, and I cannot tell you how much I miss her.

And I cannot convey the importance of a mother until she has been called home. I know my mother is with God and is watching over me. This is why your mother is also important to me.

And I have mentioned to you before that if we never meet here on this earth together. We will be together in heaven. I'm going to send you another email. I'll try to make it shorter and not as many. I do have a lot of work to do this weekend. Please tell your mother that my prayers are always with her because I care, and she is your mother who makes her even more special to me and in the eyes of God.

Thomas wrote;

Beautiful, this might sound strange, yes that's right, I said weird, smile every time I open up an email from you if it starts with the word "sweetheart." I know I am still in the ballpark like we have met before. I think some of the things I have said to you even recently, I think to myself, self, you should not be saying those things to your girl, but they are the truth.

And I would not hold the truth back from you, and some things I only think about, and when I say I think more than likely I am wrong. And I will give you a, for instance, when I mentioned to you that I thought Brian played a part in my disappearing driver's license.

I had to make sure, and Cindy stayed out in Brian's little shack last night, and she came in this morning and wanted to thank me very much. Especially after what Brian had been telling her about me, she said she just had to meet me.

And then we had a conversation together, and she gave me her telephone number in case anything happens to Brian. And she asked me if it was okay if she had my phone number. And I said I do not want you to be calling me up every day just to be talking.

I am in a relationship with a lovely young lady, and I am committed to her, and I would not do anything between you and me that I would not do in front of her. Do you understand, Cindy? And she said yes, and she said you are a man's man, and there is not too many of you out there.

I said, well, I don't know about that, and I think there are plenty of us out there; we do not know any, that's all. I also question him thoroughly about that, and I know precisely when someone tells the truth or lying to me. I could tell by their body language, and I can tell by looking in their eyes, 99% of people will not look into your eyes if they are lying to you.

Of course, there are professional liars out there who do not hesitate to look you in the eye while they are lying.

Now that my surgery has been put off, I will be at the Department of Motor Vehicles getting my driver's license Monday morning. From what I understand, I will be issued a temporary driver's license. It will just be a piece of paper with no picture on it, but I have my identification.

Now back to Cindy, she has a brother in Los Angeles that is very wealthy who supports her, and Brian just took her home in his vehicle. For the simple reason, I will not let Brian use my truck on the weekends.

Where was I? Back to Cindy, anyway, her brother is supporting her and has significant contacts with movie directors and is very successful in Los Angeles. She wanted to give her brother something as a present when he has been supporting her.

Sometimes is not what you know, it is who you know, and the combination of the two can get you to places that God would have you go. And the way I look at people I do not know, they may be a significant person in the eyes of God and someone that could positively change your life.

We never know when angels appear, so treat people accordingly because they will come as possibly a person you may not want to meet or come into contact with.

Those are usually the people that can take you to the blessings of God has to offer. Anyway, before I lose this email, sweetheart, you are my girl, and I humbles apology for writing so many emails to you.

I'm happy you let me know that sending emails takes a lot out of you, and I can well imagine. I will only send you emails, and I will document important occurrences that I feel you would like to know that transpired throughout my life until I write to you again.

You need your rest in the last thing you need to do to live mine. Life and work as hard as you are and try to survive on your own. I only make it more difficult for you by writing you many emails. I will have to read your email over and see if I have forgotten anything that you have mentioned. Course -? What's that? You mean chores, damn smile foreigners, double smile we will have fun - Tie me up? Smile.

21 October 2018

DiAnnie wrote;

> *Hey honey,*
>
> *Just a concise note to let you know that I'm thinking about you. I'm not home right now, and sorry, it seems like I'm keeping quiet or ignoring you, not so. I haven't been home, that's why since this morning. I went to church and currently visit a work friend for dinner. I'll write a lengthy message later or tomorrow. Thanks for all your messages. I know they may be much, but they mean a lot to me as well. All the voice messages too. You're so sweet, honey. Later. 💋💋 Matthew 7;13. Enter ye in at the strait gate; for wide is the gate, and broad is the way, leading to destruction, and many there be which go in thereat. 14. Because strait is the gate, and narrow is the way, unto life, and few there be that find it.*

22 October 2018

DiAnnie wrote;

> *Good morning honey!*

Thomas wrote;

> *Beautiful, you're the funniest little girl. I know I am going to spank you when I see you and am going to tickle you. Do not ever compare me with your boyfriend; first of all, I agree he was your boyfriend, second both of you met each other and knew each other spiritually. I feel that is a big difference, let me say this I am a great man.*
>
> *You realize there is nothing I would not do for you if I could with a good man.*
>
> *See what you do to me consume my mind, I'm like Adam, it's her fault she gave me the apple, smile, and you will go your name is Eve. You're talking to God, accusing God of putting the serpent in the garden; no wonder we got kicked out of the garden; it was your fault, do not take me seriously, anyway let me go back over your emails.*

I think you misunderstood me. Brian is not dying, that dumb girl Cindy wanted me to play on her sympathy, and I explained to Brian yesterday that he brought her back here.

I pray to God she does not think she is moving in. One of these days, we will become a team and work together. This I pray for. Only God knows when and I'm not pressuring you, so do not think I'm putting your head in the vice grip. In the big bench face and turning the handle and putting pressure on your head. Smile smile smile smile double backflip for a triple black flip with a full twist and 1/2 Gaynor, hugs and kisses.

Thomas wrote;

Beautiful, I'm telling you it takes to research, and I want to people to get a concept of the power of prayer in their minds, and their non-God loving liberal communist minds smile smile smile.

Please read what I have so far, and if there are any changes you would like for me to make, please do not hesitate to let me know, okay? Because you're my girl, and I prayed to God that this media questionnaire I am filling out has not made you feel in any way obligated or make me sound controlling, that was not my intent.

And I can see now that I'm looking at the mileage and all that stuff, I very well could manipulating, controlling, male macho egotistical ownership, tell the woman what to do blah blah blah. That's not who I am, sweetheart; you have taught me well, and I thank God for you in my life; hugs and kisses.

I'm learning I'm a good student; I wouldn't say I like getting ripped off by these neonates, not less I sell something. All I have to do on the media application is to finish my biography, then I can mail that in, and I can concentrate on selling some stuff around here.

I have tons of stuff to sell, I give tons of stuff away, and I still get tons of stuff. This home is excellent keep in mind, a Sgt. in the Marine Corps, and I keep my hygiene clean; I am pleased to let you know my home is clean all the time. Have a good day.

Grace and peace with God our father be with you and your mother through Jesus Christ our Lord's name amen.

25 October 2018

DiAnnie wrote;

Hello sweetheart, Thanks for all your prayers for me and my mom. They're appreciated. I feel much better today than yesterday but did not go to work. I'll go tomorrow. I have been reading all your messages, and I realize you say many things that I don't even think about and ask why you say that.

One example that you realize that I don't talk about God anymore. Are you trying to take God's place to be my judge?

One thing you didn't know before saying that is when we first met, we were just friends, and it was more like Christian friends that just met, so I mostly addressed those emails in the way of a friendship rather than intimacy.

I never turn my back to God for any reason, and I don't think I'll ever do that because I have been chosen by a price that can't be revoked. Have you ever come across something called eternal security? It is after a person has been saved.

I can't lose my salvation because I have been born again. It's like your parents giving birth to you, and they think you're not doing the right things. Can they be able to take you back in your mother's womb? No, that's the same with being born again through the salvation of Christ. So know there's nothing that can separate me from God, not even myself. I'm sorry if you feel like I'm going far away from God, not really. That might just be how you think.

Since you didn't hear from me for a day, you have started thinking negatively as you usually do. You think I am avoiding, which brought you for thinking such. Thomas, I know you so much more than you think. You're busted! 😃 Old Zoro believes I don't know.

You were just jealous. Tell me it's not true. I'm not busy, and I'm not taking a break from you unless you want that, and if so, you must have a plan hidden somewhere. You think I'm busy doing what? Not writing for a day or two made you believe that way! I had pain in my knees, that's why. You don't believe me, right? You must learn how to trust your partner. You say it, but not from your heart.

I know it's when you're not hearing from me you become like that, correct? Enjoy your day Mr. From your wife, Mrs. Stay blessed in Christ! Let Him lead us and not give the devil a chance. The devil is that negative part of our hearts that bring sadness. So I'm praying for you as well. I think it is dumb for someone to put money first in a relationship. I think the most critical thing in any relationship is love.

I understand what you mean, and men are very good at that to be like saints from the beginning, but as soon as they know all about you, they become different people. You know so much of what women go through, and my heart is already falling for you.

I have been talking much about you to my mom and showed her your picture and messages the very recent ones though not from the start..lol and she thinks you're looking for the same thing I'm also looking for, so I must continue to correspond with you and should be putting everything in prayers. She said you're an honest heart looking, minded person. She encourages me not to look at age but as a character. So who knows, we must be lucky!

27 October 2018

DiAnnie wrote;

Hello sweetheart, It seems like ages since you last hear from me and I heard from you too. I'm always thinking about you and never feel you've been forgotten. How are you doing? I hope everything is going great with you. My knees are pretty in good shape now. Whenever there's rain or cold, it happens not every time, though.

I hope you're not going to be bothered whenever it starts. Anyway, I would get better treatment from the hospital there, so I believe my situation will be better. I didn't realize how much we have written to one another! It is interesting to me writing to such a sweet person like yourself, so I didn't have time if it was huge or not.

Well, I don't doubt your love for me. I know you did mine from the beginning, but like I used to say, I wouldn't blow my own trumpet, meaning character speaks louder than how someone feels about you, left with you to prove or disprove someone about their perception of you. When I love someone, it is forever unless that person pushes me away.

Now you hello, sweetheart, it seems like ages dancing last year from me, and I heard from you to realize my heart has never changed with all we been through. I feel glad you love me too. You are proud of me. To answer your question, when I say you're jealous of me, I simply mean when you don't hear from me, you say a lot of negative things, which makes me conclude that you're. I hope you understand. I feel pressured, as you probably think, not getting back to you right away. I maybe am turning back on you or involved with someone else. Believe me. I'm not giving up on you!

Those friends I have are not going to be the person I'll get married to! Right to be around people sometimes, but I don't let anyone influence me. My mentor is my mother, and I don't think she means wrong in my life. I think it's why you like us because she gives me advice as if I was her.

She wouldn't let me go astray. Sure, you're always in my dreams, you're the only one I want in my dreams, you're the only one that matters to me after Mom! Do you wonder why a good-looking young lady falls in love with a handsome man? The question explains itself! First, it's not the attractive part but the inner beings that make me fall in love.

Suppose I was considered good-looking mostly than I should have thought, like the worldly people looking at physical appearances. I think it's a God-given realization. My mom didn't know a human was being called Thomas! 😄 *she only gave me advice as a good Mom. It seems like you have many errands to run, from the funeral to taking your wheelchair for repair on Monday. Is it your old one?*

Thanks for your last message to me; it is very encouraging. Thanks so much for all the good thoughts about me and prayers for Mom and me, all our love and prayers for you as well. Enjoy your night, my dear. Kisses 😘 *and hugs* 🤗*.*

29 October 2018

Thomas wrote;

I'm sending a picture of the gentleman I attended the funeral service for; it was 92 years old, and nobody I ever knew had a harsh word about him. This was at my mother's funeral service at the cemetery high up on a hill overlooking the lovely location. He had maintained the cemetery for years and raised a giant American flag in town every day.

Anyway, I told the story, and everybody laughed; regardless, I proceed to get drunk with this friend of mine who was married to his daughter at the time.

I drank one quart of Jack Daniels and two six-packs of beer. I was never so sick, and all my life. I said I was not in good shape and that we proceed to get into his car and spin hookers around the house through the Rose Garden, through the hedges, across the lawns, through the close line, etc. broke a screen door off his home and broke a big window, and my friend was living with his in-laws.

He just scratched his head and very slowly stood somebody's going to have to pay for this, and that cost $35 that was $17.50 apiece a lot at that time. Everybody enjoyed that, and then I said condolences to the family as I looked at them sitting in the front row.

I proceeded to tell Jesus started his sermon on the Mount with the nine Beatitudes in the book of Matthew chapter 5 verse three says blessed that they who mourn, so they shall be comforted. Then I said, also Jesus sermon on the Mount chapter 6 verse nine through 13 is the Lord's prayer in Jesus Christ our Lord says the word heaven twice in that prayer. I started another Bible verse, second Corinthians chapter 5 verse eight, Jesus says to be absent from the flesh is to be present with the Lord.

Brian, who was supposed to be pushing me in my wheelchair, as it will be upfront. I'm going to say something, Brian said, you're kidding, right, about 150 people or more standing room only, I said I am not joking let's go. He reluctantly pushed me upfront, and I told the above, and then Brian was not right behind me to take me back.

I said to everyone I could stay up here and talk longer if you care for me too; I smile, and everybody clapped and said, please go ahead, don't stop now. Anyway, it was fun having the Holy Spirit work through me to say what I had to say, and when I know the Holy Spirit works through me, I do not know what's going to come out of my mouth. I think about it afterward, and I thank God for the words that come from my mouth.

I want to thank my guardian angel for writing such a beautiful email to me. That means a lot to me, and I do appreciate that; I thank God for you.

Monday, the gentleman who is coming out to fix my electric wheelchair, I will see if I can get him to fix my old electric wheelchair; I need to get that fixed before selling it, so say your prayers.

I can and understand beautiful, and I will not lie to you only the truth, to lie to you about that God would not answer one of my prayers. Not being able to take care of this beautiful guardian angel that God sent to me would mean a trip to hell or reprimanded severely by God this I know.

Brother Brian for losing my driver's license, it all happens for a reason, I guess, maybe so I could go into the Department of Motor Vehicles and make about 200 people forget about the trials and tribulations for the day. I do not know God's mind as none of us do, I can only say that everything happens for a reason, and it happens for a very spiritual reason in my life. I was thinking about you today. I should say I was thinking about us together and what a dynamic God-given gift we will give to others through our presence together. Whenever that happens, it will be God's time, not mine, not when I want it to happen, or not when you want it to happen. It will just happen when God wants to. And your mother, I pray for her daily because she is a blessing from God.

I know that she is your mentor in your life, and your mother has great spiritual advice because of her wisdom and knowledge of God. And for that, I thank God for my guardian angel and her mother, and it says in the Bible we each have two guardian angels, another coincidence? I don't think so. God knows I need to Guardian Angels, so he sends you my beautiful girl and her gracious mother as my guardian angels. And for that, I cannot thank God enough, grace and peace from the Lord, our father be with you and your mother through Jesus Christ our Lord's name amen.

You're my girl. You're my guardian angel. I'm in love with you because of the angel you are xoxo.

Thomas wrote;

Beautiful, if we do not return to the righteous morals of the Bible, we will not be a family, a man who loves his wife; they have their children and call that a family. This family as we know it will disintegrate if we do not return to; thou shall not have any other gods before me. We shall survive with our love for one another. This is the word of God our Father through Jesus Christ our Lord's name. I pray these prayers for your mother and yourself.

We are not perfect, but we must build our love based on how we came together equally yoked spiritually. 2 Corinthians 6; 14. Be not unequally yoked together with unbelievers; for what fellowship has righteousness with unrighteousness? And what communion has light with darkness? 17. Wherefore come out from among them, and be ye separate, saith the Lord, and touch not the unclean thing; and I will receive you.

What you are willing to walk away from, maybe what God is ready to bring you to. It would be best if you walked away from the darkness before you can embrace the light.

That is the foundation our love was built on. I pray to God the spiritual foundation will survive between the two of us so we can lead many others into the presence of God our father, this you and I pray together, and we hold and honor our love with trust, consideration, compassion, and the joy that we will experience together one day. Because you are my girl and I'm in love with you, God and your mother love you. Hugs and kisses.

DiAnnie wrote;

Hello My love,

It's always a pleasure hearing from you, and looking at the picture must've been sad to lose a friend. 92 seems a lot of years, but no one ever gets tired of living, so it's unfortunate to me. You're a people person, and people seem to be carried away by your sense of humor and wisdom! All you said at the funeral was touching, and many people must've felt sad hearing the story many years ago. These times bring back memories! You guy Brian, and you must make people laugh all the time. Whenever I read about the two of you, I say, wow, these two guys will never change from making people laugh.. trust it, be laughing at you two when I come down there ☺. Please keep a smile, you two. I like how you get along! Well, honey, I know God sent me to guide you through, and same with you to guide me through. We both should never get tired of each other no matter what. I'm not going to ever turn my back on you.

You prove to me that you're a man and can take care of me. Man care is not the same as that of a woman, but I promise to take care of you in our life journey. I genuinely love you, and you genuinely love me.

I'm concerned about your well-being as well. You can take pictures of them and send me to see someone out there just like them. I like how you reason, babe. You don't blame others for their wrongs. After being it good or bad, God allows all people don't seem to realize that. Instead of blaming Brian, you rather thank him because you had the opportunity to meet those people at the auto office. You're such an intelligent person! I hope you had a great day. Mine was great as I had the opportunity to go to church today. I feel renewed in the spirit and all praise to God. Enjoy your time till I hear from you once again. You're my love forever. Be blessed with the love of our Lord Jesus Christ. Hugs and kisses 😘.

CHAPTER 6

Romantic Memoirs from Heaven

November 2018

4 November 2018

Thomas wrote;.

> *Beautiful, I pray to God you are doing well, and I understand; I have got my driver to license back. One day, please let me know how you are doing? I feel no news is good news. Of course, that is always not true. I'm in love with you. I love you. God bless with prayers. My Northern girl hugs and kisses.*

DiAnnie wrote;

> *Hi sweetheart,*
>
> *I was waiting to get a message from you before writing. In one of your voicemails, you said you were going to write me an email, but before then, you needed some rest since you're back from the hospital. That's why it seems like I am keeping quiet. Apart from that, you're always in my prayers. How is the pain now? I hope that everything is going well, and I like you to know that you're continually in my prayers. Mom has been praying for you as well. You have a loving family here that cares much for you.*

I saw the conversation between you and the girl from the site. It good you noticed the difference between a couple of them and me. Like I always told you, I don't try to impress anyone or change for anything for any reason. I'm preferred just to be me, not anyone. I don't think I'll befriend someone that behaved rudely to you. I got a few friends I'm struggling with to get them away from me, so imagine a new friend.

You're my best friend, for now, you and my beloved Mom, and that's fine for me. Since you told me about this girl contacting you, I have myself wondering what the hell this Zoro still doing on a dating site? I deleted myself from there as soon as I knew you were the person I would love, so no one else contacts me, but you are still there, and believe me, that's not fair to me. Think about moving out of there.

You said Mom knows about your surgery? I think that's cool because, in life, someone closer to you must know about you no matter what. It's only left to keep things to them because it's not nice to put someone's secrets out to other people. After all, that person trusted you. So tell him that I say no blah blah out there about what you have done. It's nothing even to be ashamed of because you're doing it for me and your children I will have for you.

! Lol bad boy 😀. *I am looking forward to hearing from you. Enjoy the rest of your day. With the love of the Lord, stay blessed. Your endless love* ♡.

5 November 2018

Thomas wrote;

Beautiful, your consumption of my life and time will always be cherished in my *heart, my mind, and my soul because of God's love and the love of God. There are several types of love, the if kind of love, if you buy me a car, I will love you, if you send me money I will love you, if you can provide for me substantially for the rest of my life I will love you.*

Then there is the because it's love because you are good-looking and intelligent. I will marry you because you are successful and have a lot of money. I will love you. There is God's love, despite your not having any money, I love you, despite you not being successful I will love you, despite you having one arm and multiple sclerosis, I will love you, despite everything you have done in the past, with all your faults and all of your mistakes and all of your dreams that were crushed, I will love you.

Despite myself and you, I will always love you. Laying back, dreaming, and praying to God, the answers flood my mind and between thoughts of you and me together. And that may or may not happen. If we were meant to be together, we would have been together by now. Nothing stops this man from accepting his Northern girl and taking care of her and loving her and working with her and making our life together at present.

Inspired of our miraculous love together so far, and beyond my comprehension or imagination, it only had to come through a prayer of which has have happened—in my mind, sincerely working together on this project that will be far more lucrative for us and blessings from God beyond our comprehension or imagination.

I will always care about your mother because I know in my heart she has prayed for someone like me to come into your life. And to deprive your mother of that is also a sin. If this is all about you and your needs and only your needs, you can count me out. I'm not interested in God's blessings that will surpass our imagination when we work together. I love you for who you are, my Northern girl.

Please talk this over with your mother and let me know what you decide? The decision is yours, beautiful, realizing you have your own life to live and choosing to live it with your friends and your work is an excellent decision on your part, and I am proud of you, although that's not who I am and I do not care to grovel for crumbs that fall off of someone's table. You know, tips working by the hour just getting by, that's not God's intentions for me or us if you so choose.

And this is where the age difference may affect or become detrimental to our relationship, I know you are at the age where your friends are vital, and you feel that they are your best friends, and I'm sure they are. On the other hand, I do not see any of them helping you or have not mentioned it to me.

I do not want to stress you. I do not want to worry you. All I want is for you to be happy. I am offering you a life of happiness that you can be proud of because God will be working with us together through Jesus Christ, our Lord.

This I have been told, and I choose not to pass up this opportunity I cannot wait any longer; I must get to work, so the emails and telephone calls will and please do email me, and I will respond, and if you care to call me on the telephone, please do.

A true story I heard tonight, a minister visited a cancer ward and noticed a very tall, good-looking gentleman 6 foot two, dark wavy beautiful hair strikingly handsome, with this little seven-year-old boy with a shaved head because of chemotherapy. The minister went back about two weeks later, and noticed that the good-looking gentleman was bald and had absolutely no hair, the little seven-year-old boy holding his daddy's hand, said to the minister, look, my dad shaved his head. We are going to let our hair grow back together. That's love. That's God's love.

7 November 2018

Thomas wrote;

Matthew 12:25

Knowing their thoughts, he said to them, "Every kingdom divided against itself is laid waste, and no city or house divided against itself will stand. Mark 3:25

And if a house is divided against itself, that house will not be able to stand. 1 Corinthians 1:10

I appeal to you, brothers, by the name of our Lord Jesus Christ, that all of you agree and that there be no divisions among you, but that you be united in the same mind and the same judgment.

8 November 2018

Thomas wrote;

Can you make good decisions and be right all the time? We might try to establish a few rules for romance apical across most cultures. Adam and Eve were given one authority by God our father and could not keep it. Let us try this; do not flirt with someone unless you might mean it. Do not pursue people who you're not interested in or who are not interested in you.

In general, expressed your affection or uncertainty clearly, unless there is a particular reason not to. Love is the natural divine drive as powerful as hunger. Women are susceptible to status and security. Men are sensitive to youth and beauty.

These differences are part of a natural selection process where males seek many healthy women of childbearing age to mother offspring, and women seek men who are willing and able to take care of them and their children.

A force "romantic attraction," which is a combination of genetic and cultural factors. This force may be weak or strong and may be felt to different degrees by each of the two love partners. The other aspect is "emotional maturity," which is the degree to which a person can provide adequate treatment in a love relationship.

Thus, an immature person is more likely to overestimate love, become disillusioned, and have an affair. In contrast, a mature person is more likely to see the relationship in realistic terms and act constructively to solve problems.

Considers romantic love as a "commitment device" or mechanism that encourages two humans to form a lasting bond has explored the evolutionary rationale that has shaped modern romantic love and has concluded that long-lasting relationships are helpful to ensure that children reach reproductive age and are fed and cared for by two parents.

The fantasy bond, which is what is mostly created after the passionate love has faded. A couple may start to feel comfortable with each other to the point that they see each other as only companions or protectors, but yet think that they are still in love with each other. The results of the fantasy bond are the leading to companionate love.

They studied college students in the early stages of a relationship. They found that almost half reported that their significant other was their closest friend, providing evidence that passionate and companionate love exists in new relationships.

Conversely, in a study of long-term marriages, researchers found that couples endorsed measures of both companionate love and passionate love and that passionate love was the strongest predictor of marital satisfaction, showing that both types of love can endure throughout the years.

However, a study published in the journal Proceedings of the National Academy of Sciences in 2012 looked at about 19,000 married people. Those who met their spouse online said their marriage was more satisfying than those who met their spouse offline. Plus, marriages that began online were less likely to end in separation or divorce.

The average life expectancy has been rising, leaving many young singles feeling as if they have plenty of time to find a <u>life partner</u>. This opens up time to travel and experience things without the burden of a relationship. As of 1996, more than 20% of Northerns "were not living in the same census subdivision as they were five years earlier," and as of 1998, more than half of employed Northerns worried "they [did] not have enough time to spend with their family and friends."

"Social networking service" is a broad term, branching out to websites based on many aspects. One aspect that is possible on all social networking sites is the possibility of an internet relationship. These sites enable users to search for new connections based on location, education, experiences, hobbies, age, gender, and more.

This allows individuals to meet each other to have some characteristics in common already. These sites usually allow people who do not know each other to "add" each other as a connection or friend and send each other messages. This connection can lead to more communication between two individuals.

An immense amount of information about the individuals can be found directly on their social network profile. Proving those individuals include plentiful and accurate information about themselves, people in online relationships can find out much about each other by viewing profiles and "about me's."

Communication between individuals can become more frequent, thus forming some type of relationship via the internet. This relationship can turn into an acquaintance, a friendship, a romantic relationship, or even a business partnership.

9 November 2018

Thomas wrote;

Rejection leads to resentment and a wounded spirit; it can poison your mind, rob you of joy, robbed you of peace and self-confidence and hope for your future, Proverbs 18; 14 the soul of a man will sustain him in sickness, but you can bear a broken spirit?

Rejection can be the sense of being unwanted, you want people in your life to love you, but you believe they do not love you. They never will love you, you never felt the love of your mother as a child, you felt the betrayal of your mother, you never felt the love and acceptance from your father, he gave you his name and a place to live, and food to eat but he never gave you himself. You have holiness with Christ through the blood at the cross.

My girl from The North Country, and please try not to feel rejected. That will lead to resentment and a wounded spirit. It could rob you of joy, peace, self-confidence, and hope for the future. I'm proud of you DiAnnie, you will always be my girl, and you will always be my best friend.

And I pray to God for you that you find that love in your life that we have online, do not stop praying and believing in a love that you so deserve, I will always be your friend, and for now, can we please just look at it as a friendship like penpals.? And not depend on each other for anything, just friends needing advice from time to time or someone to talk to honestly.

I'm not going anywhere just yet that I know of, and living alone all these years, and you tapping me on the shoulder and introducing yourself as the beautiful young lady that you are, was quite courageous. And for that, you should be commended and congratulated because you happen to tap one of God's children on the shoulder, and you do not believe in miracles?

I know you do you have told me, nothing happens perchance remember. So two of God's children have met one another as friends and overextended their friendship into a deeper understanding and meaning of what it was, without either of us knowing it at the time.

And we have known each other for eight or nine months now and have communicated quite frequently. And we are each looking for the same thing, I believe, a love that neither of us has ever had before. And do not ever stop looking for that love, because I never will, with my unshakable faith and keeping a positive, loving outlook on life, not harmful, worry or stress.

And please understand that I grew up with a father and mother who just loved their children unconditionally. My father always somehow managed to bring the family together, because we all loved one another even though we did not have much.

Most of the time, there was no food in the house, almost all the time, we got kicked out of the house as we were in, one house we had to drill holes in the floor to let the water out the roof leak so bad. It seemed we always had to find a place to live. My mother worked three jobs to keep food on the table for five children, my dad drank up every penny he made, plus stealing from my mother.

But there was always a sense of love in our family. As bad as things seem to have been, there was still that love unconditionally.

Not the perfect love because none of us are perfect. This is not an ideal world. We cannot part the Red Sea or walk on water. And we are continuously going to make mistakes that only strengthen our spiritual love for God and Jesus Christ to get to heaven one day.

Where you and I will be reunited is far beyond my comprehension or understanding at times; all I can do is keep reading the word of God and listening to my ministry shows on YouTube.

I hunger for the word that will make me that perfect person that will walk right into heaven one day.

Proverbs 18; 14 – the spirit of a man will sustain him in sickness, but who can bear a broken heart? Rejection can be the feeling of being unwanted. You want people in your life to love you, but you believe they do not love you, and they never will love you.

Please do not feel any guilt for picking up one of God's broken children; I pray to God that it has only strengthened your ability and what you would desire in the future. I will always be here for you as a friend with no expectations.

And I also pray to God that you have become stronger as a beautiful young lady and what you would want as far as love and a future relationship goes. Because I care, and I would have to be crazy to think that you did not make a better man out of me, is the reason who I am today. And once again, can you please forgive me for overextending our friendship and leading you to believe that everything was going to be okay? I always think that, though I still believe everything will be okay, and they usually are, if I state out of my way.

You also made me realize that it is not pleasant to take advantage of another person's feelings who cares for me. And for this, I thank you because stepping on someone else's feelings is most certainly not a godly thing to do. I'm broken, yet bit by bit, piece by piece. I pray that God will bless us together one day. I am willing to grow along spiritual lines like I have mentioned before do the next right thing. With care, your friend from the United States and Arizona.

Postscript; "soulmates from heaven" is on hold and may remain that way because I'm finding soulmates do not come from heaven. They go to heaven.

I'm going to take a gospel trip. I'm a-gonna take a trip. In the good old gospel ship, I'm goin' far beyond the sky. I'm a-gonna shout and sing. Until all the Heavens ring, When I bid this old world goodbye. I have good news to bring, And that is why I sing.

All my joys with you I'd like to share, Oh, I'm a-gonna take a trip. In the good old gospel ship, And go sailin' through the air. Oh, I can scarcely wait; I know I don't want DiAnnie to be late. For I want to spend all my time in prayer, And a when my ship comes in, I'm a-gonna leave this world of sin And go sailin' through the air.

10 November 2018

Thomas wrote;

As hard as I could with my shoe, I kick myself in the face, knocking all my teeth out. I kick myself as hard as I could rite in the balls, then I pick myself up again, body-slammed myself on the floor, kick myself in the eye, and I apologize for being so mean to myself in front of you.

I bet you did not even feel sorry for me, did you? I didn't. I enjoyed it. I think I would do it again tomorrow, and every day after that, until you realize that I care about you. I would never betray you or destroy our friendship under any circumstances; no matter how hard you try to reject me, I will always be here for you as a friend.

After hearing that her dream through God's grace, Thomas informed DiAnnie was to have two children. He decided to have it reversed for a reason. Thomas also wanted children with DiAnnie.

DiAnnie being an orphan and DiAnnie's mother Anna being a widow, this small family's small nucleus has so much love for one another.

Anna DiAnnie's mother is aesthetic and divinely overwhelmed with respect, kindness, and appreciation for this child. A first-time grandmother, Thomas, and DiAnnie can only imagine what it must feel like for Anna to have a grandchild finally. Keep God first and pray.

Thomas wrote;

And have your place to stay when we are there in France, no commitment, no obligation, and please do not feel that you have to accept; God bless with prayers Thomas

beautiful, I have to reread that email, you and I both know that the reason we have been talking this long is not that I want you out here to be a love object.

I believe we both know this in our hearts because of God's will for us, and we have to look at the positive side of both of us, vasectomy reversal; thank you in my heart and my spirit. I would have never even thought of this if it were not for our meeting. You have made me a better man because of meeting you, and you are right about one thing when you say, "that I do not understand," and not being in a relationship for this many years.

I'm only putting my teeth back in, so I can kick them out again. LOL, see what you make me do, quadruple smile. I'm not sure if this is making me a better man because of you,? That I pick myself up and slammed myself on the ground kick myself in the groin take my teeth to outbreak my ribs jump up and down on my legs, then picking myself up, setting myself on the chair as nothing happened, LOL smile,

you're my girl, and I'm in love with you. I believe we both know this, and God for sure knows this. We have to be nice to each other, and you know in your heart my forgiveness is always to you because of this overwhelming love that overtakes the both of us through the grace and peace of God our Father to you and your mother through Jesus Christ our Lord's name amen.

12 November 2018

DiAnnie wrote:

Hi Thomas, I have gotten all your messages and missed calls. I think you, most of the time, don't try to understand a woman's heart. Excuse me, but I think you have lived *like this all your life, and I feel you're not realizing, have you always treated your women you have been within your past relationships good at all? If so, why have you being in different relationships?*

My not continuing communication the other day on the phone wasn't, but of the things, you said in your emails and that you were telling me on the phone.

I thought our relationship would be one of love, affection, and caring for one another. The age difference between us does not bother me; I see it as a God-given opportunity to show love to you, and you do the same. I want to take care of you as not just an old disabled person but one to spend the rest of my life with and raise our children together.

It hurt me to let you out of my life after all these months of good relationships and conversations. I'm closer to you more than anyone right now and

I think you see that as my weakness; one reason I'm writing you and forgiving you is that that's what God wants, not what I want. I have discussed this with Mom, and she told me that it is not supposed to be happening between us to stress each other. Do you think I like it when we both are hurting? Not really, I'm not a person that likes hurting others, especially such a good person like yourself, I know you're not a bad person, but there are bad things you sometimes say not knowing you told them, why do you that?

I know I'm not perfect, too. I have my pessimistic side of life; if not, then I'm not human. I know I am made perfect by the works of Christ, but I'm still human, not an angel, and it's only an honest person that can realize his or her faults and speak out. I was wrong for hanging upon you, which I ask for you to forgive me. You want us to be friends, that another thing I read in your message, and I know it's not from your heart, and if I say yes, I want only a friendship, I'll be telling a lie too because it's not from my heart as well.

Thomas, I have known you for the last time, and it's like I have known you forever, you're just that old Zoro I known since months ago, and I know as you're reading this you're laughing hard because you know I'll forgive you right? Don't be too excited when I start living with you. I'll tie you up and punish you. When you know, I'm a marine just as you only didn't go to war, and I don't know why I love this man. I know you love this silly girl too. Do you want to go to France?

Well, maybe a good idea because Mom is going over there soon, and she wanted me there, just still contemplating what to do. A lot is going on right now. It would be great to be there with you. Let's see what happens. Are you severe? You kicked yourself and took your teeth out? And throw yourself on the ground? You have me laughing 😆 replace these teeth before I meet you. If not, you'll be ashamed because they're adorable!

I pray that nothing will come between us to hate each other, we have gone a long way, and I know we love each other. I love you, and I'm not in the position to let you go either.

As long the both of us are happy, the more attractive we are to each other. I am figuring out our meeting soon, so pray as I do the same here. I am looking forward to hearing from you soon. I have forgiven you, and you do the same for rudely hanging upon you the other day. Enjoy the rest of your day. Much love from me. Hugs 🤗 and kisses 😘😘😘

14 November 2018

Thomas wrote;

Beautiful, thank you very much for writing, and I'm pleasantly pleased, excitingly static, and divinely inspired to know that you're my girl.

I'm in love with my girl, and it hurts my heart once again that I cannot provide for you at this point peace and grace be with you and your mother through Jesus Christ the Lord's name this we pray amen.

24 November 2018

Thomas wrote;

My sweet, beautiful girl from The North Country, DiAnnie, understands your necessities and needs and desires for survival. I'm facing the same situation. This is how I live from day to day, but I know everything will be okay. Have you ever thought that maybe God wants you and Me together before he performs his miracles and pours out his blessings of abundance on us?

Remember what Jesus said, "any house divided amongst itself shall not stand." Jesus did not say that for the fun of it; I just have this feeling with my unshakable faith that God will pour out his overabundance of blessings on us if we were together. Mark 3; 25. And if the house is divided against itself, that house cannot stand.

This is what I believe? We have to have goals together for the future, and it is not a bad thing to look into the future. Of course, I realize the present situation is challenging. You are the wife of a Marine.

I know you are tough, and when the going gets tough, the tough get going. I do not mean to say these things to hurt your feelings or say that I do not care because you know I do. I love you so much, and I'm in love with you so much. We are so compatibly in love according to God's grace it would be hard to ignore our love for one another.

And not to want to be with one another. And it will be God's will, and God knows the answer before prayers before we even ask. I'm praying and fasting. I'm working out, I am an excellent cook, by the way, smile. I would love nothing better than to cook you a meal because you are my girl.

I do not mean to argue because I do not think our relationship would be built on sand; Satan wants us to divide. I will not let that happen through the grace of God. We together are two bright lights that have come together as one, and no darkness should come between us or anything negative.

Any worry or stress, keep that faith, keep that happiness and a smile on your face; everything is okay right now. The next moment is not here yet, so do not go there. That's where Satan would like you to go into a depression, or to split our love apart would make the devil happy.

I will pray to God as I continued to fast and work out, talk to your mother, and peace and grace of the Lord be with you and your mother through Jesus Christ our Lord's name. It just hurts my heart. All I can do is pray, and God talks to me through the Holy Spirit, and God's will be done for the both of us, and that nothing comes between us, you are my girl hugs and kisses.

Beautiful, forgetting God, these are a couple of scenarios that I have just heard of people who forgot about God.

The perfect couple had the ideal house, who had the perfect two children and are now going through the perfect divorce. Then there was the businessman the stock market fell; he woke up a millionaire and went to bed without anything.

Paganism is plagiarism, equals Self-satisfaction, the worship of pleasure. It is as old as the Garden of Eden, the fruit so delicious and enticing. You cannot satisfy your carnal senses, thrills without, addictions were out, then your life becomes dull and mundane.

The more you have to have is, the less you're going to have. As soon as you let it go, God will provide for you. This I know from experience. As soon as you say, God, please help me, and let it go entirely out of your mind, that's when the miracle happens; faith without works is dead; you must have the dedication and keep that faith. James 2; 18. A man may say, thou hast faith, and I have works; show me thy faith without thy works, and I will show thee my faith by my works.

I pray that I must trust God to answer my prayers as he sees fit. I pray that I may be content with whatever form that answer may take through the grace of God and my faith.

God may be trying to get your attention by turning you in a new direction. One that has been in front of you, and you neglect to recognize it, think about it, please. I say these things because I care about you, and I love you; I am in love with you.

Yet you do not recognize the miracle, and I feel God keeps us both down until we come together. And I say this not to pressure you, or put anything on you, or squeeze your head in a vice.

These are suggestions I would like you to think about, and God would be pleasantly pleased if you did, and I'm not talking out of control or manipulation.

I have just been looking at our relationship and our love for one another that God has brought together through the both of us. He has brought us together. Once again, I have said this to you before.

Do you think what God has brought together he will destroy? I do not think so; we will never reach true happiness or the potential of blessings in abundance that God has in store for us. Think about what I am saying; what the Holy Spirit is working through me lets us both know. I want you to be happy. I pray for your happiness because I'm in love with you; you are my girl.

Matthew six; 33 – Jesus said to seek the first kingdom of God, and the rest will be blessed and installed on to you, Psalms 9; 17 – all nations that forget God shall be turned into a living hell.

Behind every good man, there is a great and phenomenal woman. I have never had now that I have the opportunity and yourself to have everything we need in abundance. Please, please give it a try and do not let the dream slip between our fingers. You might have regrets one day if I did not inform you of the way I feel about us.

And I feel God feels the same way; I'm in love with you. I will give my life for you, and I will do anything and everything for you, and God knows that. We will be one happy couple together when we come together, at your convenience, not mine. And when the spirit moves us together, that's when we will go together.

Peace and the grace of the Lord be with you and your mother through Jesus Christ our Lord's name, amen.

Ephesian 3:20, Concentrate on the first sentence...…"The will of God will never take you where the Grace of God will not protect you." Something good choice happens to you today — something that you have been waiting to hear. That is my prayer for you today.

For the souls who never thought that God could or would work in our lives, those who pray together stay together. Thomas is a Christian and only through the Grace of God and praises the Lord for that.

Perfection is a set-up for disappointment. This is not the Garden of Eden, and everything happens for a reason; giving and receiving is a two-way street.

25 November 2018

DiAnnie wrote;

> *Hi Honey,*
>
> *Good to hear from you once again. I read through all your messages, and believe me, I truly understand your situation and be honest with you.*
>
> *Okay, I'm not one of those, even if you try to think that low about me. You have to notice that I'm an understanding person, and you would never have any girl or lady who will be understanding as I am or have a personality of mine, one that loves you for who you are and is patient with you.*
>
> *God brought us together and has a plan even if we are near or far. God knows I'm in another geographical location, and you too, and with trust and patient with one another is how we know we are compatible.*
>
> *So please stop putting your thoughts in place of God. God wants us to be happy. That's why He brought us together. I noticed that you feel since it was me that messaged you first during our first encounter.*
>
> *Then she's just a girl who brought herself to you, so why think she will ever change her mind! You're the wrong, sir, as long as I feel I'm being pressured or not taken seriously. I can bring myself back, so understand that. If you don't wish to hurt my feeling with things you sit and write to me, then you're not supposed to say these in the first place!*
>
> *Now I am trying to be afraid of continuing in this relationship. Thomas, you're a nice person, but your utterances to a lady are very harmful. You still don't know how to treat a lady the way she expects. Believe you have struggled with this all your life, and I try to accept these negativities from the start. I saw you were changing, but then there's a saying that goes that says, "you can tell a person to throw away what is in their hand but not what is inside them."*
>
> *It's not my intention to have us divided or anything coming between us. My only problem is a man not taking his girl he claims to love seriously, not taking care of her for months. Prayers are perfect but seeing a person drowning and instead of helping them and say hey, peace upon you, is dead prayers and dead faith!*

And many Christians are very good at that. Thanks for the pictures of the nun. Please give me an update about her visit, not sure she's already there with you.

Good for you that the girl that wrote you went away. I believe that is to prove that not many girls can fit my shoes. It's only someone that loves you dearly who can go all these months with you. Still, I think the good people in life are only appreciated just a little compare to the bad ones.

It's the good that dies young, the interest that mostly faces difficulties in their lives, and you name it. So I guess I have to start being the bad girl I was, and I'll see life will improve. Not sure God would let me because my strength lasts in Him, spiritually and physically. I'm not so strong, but God makes me the person I am today because He loves me and has chosen me out of millions of lost souls

It is easily said to tell another person that you can do anything for them or lay your life down for them when the actual situation is that there. I believe you, though, and wouldn't deny that you love me. The question is, does this come from your heart, and when I do need you in a difficult situation would you come to my rescue? If yes, this is the right time!

Thanks for your encouragement, but I don't think I'm the person these types of incentives fit. I haven't forgotten God. How can I when I have eternal security? I have been born again. No one who has been born again by the grace of the Lord can forget or be forgotten by God.

Sadly, most young people have easily considered people going astray, but believe me, Thomas, I went.

Now you're making a living with you, an issue that makes me feel there's something else running in your mind when I propose coming the other time. What did you tell me?

I agree that there is a great woman behind every man, but I don't think you appreciate this girl, and I'm getting more stress once again. You're proving to me that you're a problematic person who maybe women there are avoiding.

I may fall into your world and have the worse experience of my life, and I may think things over, I didn't have any doubt I loved you with all my heart, but now I am disappointed and would say sorry and let you go.

It's not impossible to have someone else that would understand me and what I go through, not someone who sits and utter sad things in the name of encouragement. When you realize how to treat a woman good, let me know, but for now, I will ask God for direction for my life.

I'm not angry with you. I feel with such feeling you have about me. It's what going on in your heart. If I don't speak out, you would think you're right, which isn't correct; you think about things I don't; it's not fair how you feel about me while I hear love you with all my heart.

How would you feel if it was me saying all these bad things to you? Do you think all you said would make me continue to love you? No person in their right mind would be happy when someone dear to their heart say such negative things to them.

I'm drained and stress and crying after reading all you have said. God knows my heart keeps judging me.

Have a good night.

Thomas wrote;

Otherwise, we would not have been communicating this long, and I feel you know the love we have for one another is real. The last thing I want to do is hurt your feelings or make you feel bad about yourself; you realize what breaks my heart is to hear that you cry. I'm in love with you; I keep going back to that verse any house divided against itself shall not stand.

The thought of never seeing you or being with you Or communicating with you would be very sad for me, and it would break my heart. And to come and stay with me for just one week in my mind did not make any sense.

Can you please forgive me? Once again, you are a great lady. You are a wonderful lady, your precious soul in the eyes of God. And I'm so proud of you for the lady you are, the young beautiful precious lady I adore.

Please remember that I will always think of you this way as being a sweet Guardian Angel who came into my life, dutifully sent from God to a man that is very proud of her. And I thank God for you every day in my life. You are my girl, my beautiful Northern girl DiAnnie. What on God's green earth would I do without you? I keep reading what the Holy Spirit is working through me has written about you and me, and the manuscript "soulmates from heaven," and I'm going to keep writing because it soothes my soul in a very spiritual, compassionate way.

I'm not trying to pressure you into thinking or making a decision about the two of us. All I want you to do is be happy whatever makes you happy, and I'm sure some things I have mentioned in this email do not make you happy. Those are not my intentions, but we must realize. To wake up and smell the roses that sometimes the truth hurts. And I have a hard time facing reality. Whether I can handle constructive criticism and thank that person for telling me the truth about myself, otherwise we would never change.

You know I love you, DiAnnie, you know I care about you, you know I feel that you are the greatest woman alive that has ever been put into my life and made me the man I am today.

Do you understand how precious of a soul you are to me? There is no doubt in my mind that you are a beautiful great young lady, and I am very proud of you for everything you do and who you are. It matters how you feel to me, and it certainly matters how you think of me, and you know better than to say that you are just a love object in my life, Or that's all I want you for?

If you should decide to end this relationship, this broken heart will take a long time to mend. If ever, and I'm not begging you to hang on if you feel differently. My Northern girl, beautiful DiAnnie from your man ZORO, hugs, and kisses.

Beautiful, I'm proud of you. You are a great lady, and how could I not love you when you have made me a better man than I would not be if it were not for you? It brought me closer to God knowing you.

I will write more to you later a friend of mine Bill has just walked in the door not that he is more important than you. Still, he has probably something to eat and want to talk about something, I love you, I love you, I love you, and it's not about love is the reason I would like you to have you here, and I feel you know that in your heart, hugs, and kisses.

27 November 2018

DiAnnie wrote;

Good morning Thomas,

I read all your messages, and I like you to know that I don't have anything bad against you. I just wrote to you about how I felt inside, not sure you understood all I meant, or you write back for the pleasure of writing as an author or with a change of heart towards me. I hope the visit of Bill, your friend went well and that the nun was also great. Your friends are your friends, and believe me, and I would never stop you from spending time with them. Feel free whenever the need be.

There's different big honey. Women are hurt easily compare to men. I cry the other day because I have been abused in the past, and when I see a similar thing unfolding hurts me real bad. I don't deny that we don't love each other if not, we wouldn't be communicating.

It's the love we have that we are going along, but when these negative feelings start coming up, it's worth worrying about. Some friends want this to fail to laugh at me, and I know there are people there who don't want you around a young girl like myself. Think about these, and there wouldn't be a need to fight. When the two of us break up, I know it will hurt me a lot.

However, then there's still a whole future ahead of me, that's the difference between us, love does not know boundary or age difference that is why I am love with you till now because you make me a happy girl, please don't make me change or change for the good man you're for now.

Well, whenever you have a doubt running in your mind, try always to ask me because what you're thinking may not be the case. Humans are right, but not all the time.

I have been to The North Country several times, and I wanted to work here even before I met you. The North Country is a boring place right now. Not many opportunities like here. I was there because my Mom wanted us to be together for some time, I visit home most of the time, and you know that. Why did you think that negative?

The reason I thought to come over for a week before my trip was to make you know that I genuinely want to live there at least to see me in person before I go back to live by then, my Mom would be with me, why would I go to France and never be seen again? is there something that stops people from leaving France? You see, these are things I like you to stop thinking about because such would not help us grow. Why are you insecure?

If I don't want to come there to you, I'll tell you in your face. You see why I get sad sometimes because of the way you think about me. You're off track because I don't think the way you do. I want the best for us to be happy. There are a lot of things we share in common and a lot again for our future. Why would I want to stay a week, and that's all, how would we bring our kids up? When I love someone, it is with all my heart. When you don't believe what we share, then, of course, you can think this negative way.

You are forgiven once again, and believe me, when I have to get sad things from you also, it's going to be over between us. I'm not kidding; I mean what I'm saying. Thanks for your compliments. They represent a lot to me, but I know that when a woman is fed up or pushes her to the limit, there is no choice but to find happiness elsewhere. That's not my intention unless you make me feel sad and think negatively about me. If I'm your girl and precious to you, make me feel it, not cry.

I can handle constructive criticism and never too big to realize my errors, a person that recognizes is a wise person I was brought up like that, my parent disciplined me very much, my only mistake was telling you how I feel because of the bad things you, you tried to paint me in the way of a gold digger which does not fit my character and I refused to accept such.

You know I love you and didn't say I was ending the relationship, I said when I feel pressured and being taken as if I'm some sort of a girl not wanting the best for the two of us, think about the future and all we want if you do you will understand how this girl feels.

You see again, Zoro is always looking for a fight on this poor girl. If I am all you think, please make me happy and don't have me defending myself all the time as if I have done something wrong. Think positively about your girl as she does for you that's the only way we go smoothly.

Love you and never take this for granted. Make me love you more. If you love your girl, treat her like a queen.

Love and peace from me outside are so cold and in as well make me thinking about cuddling with you.

Your endless love.

Thomas wrote;

Beautiful, I just got back from the orthodontist. I had a cracked tooth, and it was major surgery. Thank God the lady orthodontist was from Vietnam, and when is an officer in the United States Navy as a dentist,

When I know, I make the lady cry, I cry. You have given me the last chance, it seems to me, and I'm only a man, and I do not want to remind you of previous relationships you have had in the past. I'm not that man. I have not been with the lady and many years, and I asked that you please teach me because this Marine is a tough Marine. And you are right

You are my Northern girl with whom I am madly in love. I am in love with you, so if I ever say anything mean to you or hurt your feelings other than not providing for you, you know I'm a good man and a softhearted man, and it breaks my feelings to hurt your feelings if that makes sense. And to think of you ending our relationship for giving me one more chance makes me feel like I am walking on eggshells, and I cannot be totally honest with you. I'm trying my best, sweetheart. I pray to God you realize that. And I am going to mess up again because I am only a man. I know that I will hurt your feelings unconsciously or consciously. I can pray to God that I do not and try my best to be the best man I can for you.

I love writing to you because I love you, and I cannot stop thinking about you. Is that wrong? And I will try to be kind with my words and what I say to you, and that's the way it should be. You are such a beautiful woman and have so much understanding knowing my situation. Not too many ladies would even consider staying with the man who has nothing to offer.

I do not want to hurt your feelings. Let us take it one day at a time and see how life unfolds in front of us. I pray to God, and I pray to God continuously that I know things will get better and everything is okay. I do not feel good about myself, beautiful not being able to take care of myself. I'm not the kind of man I always have been able to take care of myself and many others.

And it hurts my spirit, and I get a little thought going through my head, God, am I doing any good for anybody here? Sometimes I ask God to, or is it time for me to go home? Please bring me home to heaven when I have nothing to offer others as far as helping them goes.

The orthodontist this morning called her. Doc is what all Marines call United States Navy corpsmen who patch us up into a tremendous job better than any doctors when we are on the battlefield and give her a big hug.

And I also gave her the latest book, "soul sanctuary," for the simple reason it has many military pictures in there, and she and I were talking military. And we both agreed. At least I let her know after she thanked me for serving our country. I said we should thank those who did not help. They gave us a reason to act and never looked at like that. Anyway, beautiful, I love you. I'm in love with you; God loves you.

I'm not sure what to say or what's worth saying. I realize the thought of me hurting your feelings again, for some Montaigne reason, and you just slamming the door on me would tear my heart in half as no other broken heart has experienced. And I pray to God I have not hurt your feelings, you are the greatest young beautiful lady I have ever known in my life, and God has given me a love that I have never experienced before through you, that I know for a fact it can grow beyond our wildest imagination, and never be boring and always be happy, this is what I feel.

I'm proud of you, and every word you said in your email to me was exactly true, and I will not dispute anything that you said. And I would not blame you for anything that I did that would cause you to slam the door on me. I feel that bad, I do not know what to do sometimes, you are a great woman that has met a great man. and I can understand some things I have said that must've made you feel like past relationships you have been in; I'm not that man although I acted like it I'm sure in your mind.

I'm getting repetitive. I pray to God that you can understand what I am saying and what I have said. If you cannot, it's because I am a man, and I would love to have those feelings, emotions, and intuition of a lady. Unfortunately, I do not. I will pray through Jesus Christ our Lord's name for you and your mother that you are feeling okay and that everything is going okay in your life. Please let me know how you are feeling and how you're doing? I care. I'm interested in learning about your life—hugs, and kisses with love and prayers.

Thomas wrote;

Beautiful, I'm trying to treat you like a queen. With my present financial status, how can I? I will never take you for granted, and please do not ever think of what other people think about us. We are not here to please other people. We are here to set an example and love each other, I think about you all the time, and I would love nothing better than to cuddle with you. You are my girl, and I am your Zoro, your eternal love.

Beautiful, you consume my thoughts because you are a God-given gift that I am still perplexed somewhat as to why God would grant me one of his miracles,?

28 November 2018

DiAnnie wrote;

Good morning Hun,

Glad each time we can hear from one another. I hope your day is going great so far. Mine has started ever since just thought to write you back, so you know that I got your message and not trying to ignore you.

I'm sorry you had a cracked tooth removed with your dentist. I hope it's not too bad and didn't hurt you so bad because such hurts very much. Good, you had those excellent doctors that have worked with soldiers and marines before and know how to treat you right.

I'm honored to be a part of your life at this moment of your life. If it's God will to take you home, at least you'll know there was a guardian angel called DiAnnie that came into your life to put a smile on your face, or if we both were to be called today, we would always remember the good time we have here that's the feeling I want for us not fighting or making each other to cry. You know, after all, I do make you a better person with the life you have lived in the past because if not you wouldn't have understood how important I am in your life, there is a good relationship between us that I think you see very different from all you have been into.

I put all myself into it because you are important to me, and I never bore with you. You're a fascinating person and one who is fun to be around with. God didn't make a mistake for you and me to have so many similarities even in our families, our Dad's birthdays, our lifestyle so much.

Ending this relationship to me would be like denying God's plan for both of us. I don't plan to do that, but you also should understand that pushing an innocent girl to the wall may not be the right thing to do. Making her happy and also making you happy is healthy for the relationship. It's how others appreciate and envies being like us.

Honey, with all the nice words you write to me, tells me a lot about you and how much you mean to me, you treat me like a queen, to be honest, it's only a few misunderstanding recently that made me feel confused, but I know you genuinely love me. You will continue to be the man I love and my Zoro.

Thanks for the messages, and as always, they make me happy especially know how you're doing. I look forward to hearing from you later. Enjoy the rest of your day.

Be blessed today. Your sweet DiAnnie.

30 November 2018

DiAnnie wrote;

Good evening my love,

So fair hearing from you once again, it's always a pleasure to do that. How is your day going? Honey, I know you love me and didn't mean to say you're an older man negatively..lol you know I wouldn't do that. No one likes getting old, not even me..lol.

I'm not listening to anyone, and I don't think I would give anyone reason to interfere in our affairs. Good, my Mom is in favor of you, so not much to worry about.

As long you love me, and I love you, that's all that counts to me, not how or what others feel. Good, you got the opportunity to get treated with the dentist, my love. God has many ways to make things possible for His children.

I'll be glad that people there would be happy to see us together. That's my prayer to live happily with you and not being stressed because others are not happy.

Well, not to complain, I must say things are going well as long there's life, so yes, thanks for asking. Well, as I said before, just let me know when you don't understand anything. I'll always explain to you. You're right. God brought us together out of 7 billion people. There isn't an accident, and we share many things in common as well.

There should be an avenue to earn for our lives and that of our kids, so we should be looking to that. Well, good, you can tell that I'm patient with you, not many girls would be like me, and I'm proud of my Mom for my upbringing. I do not want either of us to change but to continue to love one another until we finally are together. I promise to always be here for you too, and believe me, as long you continue to be nice to me, I'll always be the girl you have dreamed of all your life to have.

Honey, my Mom continually prays for you and me, and she only wants the best for our children and us. There's a whole future ahead of us, and it's only prayers that can bring everything to the past. You're the man of my dreams, and please don't make it fail. You're always on my mind and in my prayers and the love I have for you I have never have it for any other man, you're just the person I have wanted, and the funny thing is you're the very first older person I have dated and falling deeply in love with, tell me what you have done to me?

You're so funny, sweetheart. Do you think I'm that a tough person? I'm just a girl who has a soft heart and comfortable crying, but yeah, if you do bad things to me, I'll indeed tie you up for hours until you tell me you're not going to it again. You make me smile so much with your sense of humor. That's one reason I always look forward to hearing from you.

You make me love writing these days. I have never written so much to anyone as I have done with you, so there must be a strong connection spiritually between the two of us. I missed us talking on the phone. This silly phone makes everything so sick not hearing your voice. I need a new one. I must figure out getting a new and advance one soon. What is your carrier there? I mean, which phone company do you use. Here I use Bell The North Country.

Honey, please, Thanks for the picture of your friend, she must be a hard-working person. I can't imagine working with the president, lol. Has she left yet? I mean the nun.

Thanks for getting back to me once again, and sorry for my delay. I was so tired last night.

Have to get busy now. Love you so much, and have a blessed day, handsome man.

Regards always from DiAnnie, your girl.

CHAPTER 7

Romantic Memoirs from Heaven

December 2018

1 December 2018

DiAnnie wrote;

Hey honey!

It's great to hear from you, what's your plan for the weekend? I got a few errands to run after I finish this message to you. Not sure you remember my shop. I was operating in The North Country before coming here, there were goods in there I didn't sell, and I would like to go there and bring those items here, some jewelry,

Ah, finally, your friend left already. I wish her a safe journey. Let me know when you get a word from her. She's a lovely person and must care for you so much. Not many friends would do as she does; anyway, you're a people person.

So many people like you very much. I think it's a God gift for you, or I'll say your laughter is your secret. That's one thing I always remember about you whenever I think about you, your smile, sir..lol I always thought about the healing water at the Lourdes de France. I knew there was a secret many didn't know about. You must be lucky to know about this link she told you. I want you healed, my love, and my knees too, and we will be two happy people! Where in The North Country is the Germania? I would look for it everywhere for you believe.

That dream must have been an evil one. Good, you woke up from your sleep because I believe I would never compete with another lady to share one man. I'm a one-person lady. I hope you don't have another young girl somewhere, and you're making it a dream..lol just kidding because I would start to cry again. Pray that such dreams will go away from you, okay? Not all dreams are from the Lord. I would never want you heartbroken. That's why I pray each time for our relationship, and Mom does as well.

I will be keeping you in prayers, my love, concerning the doors that are opening for you that your book is published soon. I know God is going to put everything under control. I'm not going to stop praying till everything is fine. Once your books are making progress, it's going to be a joy for me too. Still, when there's no progress, it is when I get sad about those publishers, I guess any right-minded person would feel the same way I do. Well, yes, our books are not only for us but for our kids and grandkids. I'll contribute when I come to you for the book. You want me pregnant on my first visit?

You're right, though. That is funny but so true, that before we go to heaven we must die first, tell me how many people want to die now? Not even you or me, but it's just truth. As a marine and a marine's wife, I guess this thought shouldn't scare me, lol.

We are watching out but hey, not for 12 children! not going to produce the 12 tribes of Israel! Lol, four is cool, boys and girls, not 12. You want to kill this little girl, you Zoro! Lol, Well, my first visit wouldn't be a marriage, we can get engage then when I come for my second visit with my Mom which is going to be my stay, then we can get married, believe me, Mom would be so sad when I get married while she's not present, you know that feeling right?

Honey, it's like we think the same way, the only thing I think is sleeping in the same bed, waking up and cooking together, taking walks, and people in your area seeing the first nation and French Sicilian girl, they would be wondering who she is? You have much explaining to do to them. lol

I pray so much for the best for our lives, and I know we have a bright future ahead of us, and hoping I'll spend my birthday with you. Enjoy your day, babe, and I will go out and do some errands and looking to hear from you later.

Be blessed and kisses from me.

3 December 2018

Thomas wrote:

> *No, you do not know what it's like to be in love with somebody like you. The way that I love you, you'll never know how much I love you the way that I love you, there's a certain kind of light that shines from God above lets me see the way that I love you, and you will never know the way that I love you baby you do not know what it's like to love somebody the way that I love you with prayers and love grace and peace from the Lord above shining brightly on you and your mother through Christ is nothing but love.*

4 December 2018

DiAnnie wrote;

> *Hi, my love,*
>
> *Sorry, it has been a few days that you have not hear from me. I have been swamped and thought to write to you now. I'm doing fine, and sorry for the silence. It wasn't intentional at all.*
>
> *How have you been keeping? You're always on my mind and in my heart as well, no matter what delay that occurs.*
>
> *Ha, you think getting pregnant with triplets would straighten my knees?*
>
> *You're so funny honey, maybe you're right, lol, but hmmm, how would this slim girl be able to take triplets with this flat stomach! We will see when we get there, lol. I like your sense of humor, and it would be one reason I would never want to leave you. You know how to make me smile. That's the secret of a lady once a guy can make her smile each time. I look to us being a big happy family. My mother would love it to see us being happy.*
>
> *I will make a trip wherever the Thomas is, and then I will either post it or bring it with me when I'm coming to Arizona. It would be a great thing when the two of us can get medication for our health issues.*

I look to that so much. You asked the other day how my knee started. Well, I have had a car crashed two times, and it has affected my knees. I was much younger than. Next time she would come there, you will learn many things and maybe get some more help from her.

It's not her but God that brought her the other day just as He brought you and me together. About the 12 children, I knew you were kidding Zoro. I know with the love you have for me, you wouldn't let me suffer so much with the 12 tribes of Israel..lol You would take care of those kids but too much for me, lol.

Honey, I'm glad that God has brought us together in this life, and I'm sure in the life after death, we will be together again, so He's not finished with us yet. I know He has an excellent plan for us. If not, we wouldn't be here still loving each other. True love from God is what we are experiencing, and not many would understand because it's not a human-made love, but that centered on God's purpose. In years to come, I will look back where we came from and be thankful to God.

We have a lot in common and a lot to share as we continue to live together.

I am relieved that no one there would see me and turn their face or be harsh to us that's one feeling no one wants from others for not coming from that particular geographical location, once I am assured that we will be love when I start to live there then I am more than happy.

Well, I have always wanted to be a self-sufficient person, not to be a politician but a business person, because the wealthiest people in the world today are business people. It's not too late. There's still a future when I start sooner. Good, we share this business mindset. I don't want to depend on my husband's pocket, and right my husband supports my ideas. It means a lot to me.

Good how you respond to those ladies that you have your wife in The North Country, you are a committed husband, I have deleted my account ever since from that site, and I am not on any website so that no one can even contact me, I must focus on what we have and build on it, so I do not have any problem of people getting me.

Let's never let all this time and happiness and fun we share go down the drain for anyone; I believe establishing such love with someone else would be possible, but not like this. That's why I do not think about leaving you. We will grow and live a happy life instead of thinking about anyone or letting anything holding us down. God will never allow that. I love you so much, honey. I will try to get some sleep shortly. I'm exhausted now.

I look forward to hearing from you soon. Enjoy your time, babe.

Gros issues.

God bless.

Your northern girl.

5 December 2018

Thomas wrote:,

Beautiful, I'm in love with you. I do not mean to insinuate anything other than our love between the two of God and us with your mother, know that I love you and I always will no matter what peace and grace of the Lord be with you and your mother through Jesus Christ our Lord's name amen you're my girl.

DiAnnie wrote:

Good morning, my love. I hope you slept well and you're going to have a good day. Well, I must be that one-legged lady for sure on the kicking contest. Lol, sometimes things get hectic, but we have to make time for those we genuinely love.

I look to hearing from you to go to The North Country to get my goods. Not comfortable waiting at this time.

Thanks for being the man of my heart. I know in years to come, we will look back and be proud of our relationship. It would be nice to treat this knee once and for all. I must get busy now, my love. Hugs and kisses. Your love DiAnnie.

Thomas wrote:

Beautiful.

You sound busier than a one-legged lady at an ass-kicking contest, LOL, that does not sound like any fun to me, a big smile with a grin. Sometimes I am worthless as chalk on the board, LOL. You get the message, and I'm sure beautiful, is; one thing I do know for sure is that you are my girl from The North Country and the only one I am in love with or will ever be in love with.

I do mean that ever ever ever no one else, you are a miracle that came into my life, and I will not let the grace of God be treated lightly without prayer, love, respect, and my absolute faith that through Jesus Christ our Lord will come through in our lives at the moment of need.

How are you doing? How is your mother doing? You know what to do. I do not walk in your shoes, especially when it comes to the contest, a smile I will remove from your shoes now, or should I say shoe? And I did not mean the 12 tribes of Israel; I told the 12 apostles, smile with a big grin. We will be busy, smile with a big grin, one precious baby at a time, and I do believe your mother will agree with me upon that and sanction my beliefs.

I do appreciate you in my life. I thank God for you and your mother in my life and mostly you, my beautiful girl. You are a sweetheart. And I'm in love with you, and we are certainly going to take care of your knees. I'm not sure if being pregnant with triplets would do it? Real small smile a severe smile, we will take one day and see how things go, in the meantime know in your heart that I love you and only you, God bless with all my love, I love you.

God knows how much I love you, you are an answer to a long-awaited prayer that patiently for over the years I have been waiting for and praying for, and God knows that. You are my precious Guardian Angel, and now I am tired; it is 12:45 AM, and I just woke up to go to the bathroom and thought I would answer your letter, of which I will reread it.

And thank you so very much for all your time in writing your letters to me. Means a lot, your everything in my heart and soul. I will also send you the prayer that I prayed to God before we met, and then I'm going to read you the response to my prayer from

God working through the Holy Spirit through me to you. It is a miraculous prayer in answer to my prayer, and keep in mind this is before we ever met; it will bring tears to your eyes as it does mind every time I read it; you're my girl.

6 December 2018

Thomas wrote:

Beautiful, How are you doing? And what have you been doing? And how is your day going? Or evening? I pray to God everything is going okay, and peace and grace of the Lord be with you and your mother is always through Jesus Christ our Lord's name this I pray.

You are my girl from The North Country, and I am in love with you. I still have been and always will he, and you will always be my only girl. Is there love afterlife? Of course, there is, and there is love during this life. However, the more prophecy I study, the end time seems to be drawing nearer and nearer, so if for some God-given reason, we do not spend our life together here on this earth. We will most certainly be together in heaven, and that will be eternal. God did not put us together for no reason, and I thank God.

Please do not worry or stress that Satan wants you to do, and we do not go there, do we? I love you. I am in love with you, and God loves you, and God loves your mother, and God loves all three of us. This I know because the Bible tells me so, I'm in love with you, and I love you, and you are all I think about.

Thomas wrote:

Beautiful, I thank God for you in my life daily, and I cannot stop thinking about us together and especially about the way God has put us together in this miraculous relationship. Peace and grace of the Lord be with you sweetheart through Jesus Christ our Lord's name to make sure let your mother know that my prayers are with her as well you are my girl in The North Country. I'm in love with you.

DiAnnie wrote:

> *Good morning honey,*
>
> *It's always my pleasure to hear from such a sweet man. How are you doing this morning? I hope you had a good night's sleep since you were very busy yesterday. My day is about to get active again, so I write you this message better and get going.*
>
> *I have to hurry now. I will write you more later during lunch. I just wanted to get back to you so you know I'm fine.*
>
> *Hugs, my sweet man. Your endless love from God.*

7 December 2018

Thomas wrote;

> *Beautiful – I pray things are going well for you, sweetheart, and your mother as well. I realize you are a very busy lady, especially during the holiday seasons, and I know in my heart you will bring a lot of joy and happiness into others lives on this holiday season, so take comfort that you are doing God's will by making others happy and joyous this holiday season.*
>
> *These are blessings only an angel can bring into others' lives. A guardian angel sent into my life with appreciation and love from my heart and heaven above.*
>
> *I will be devoting a lot of my time this weekend, so please let your mother know as well as yourself to say prayers. They are very important in God's eyes, showing our love for him through Jesus Christ, our Lord's name.*
>
> *His only begotten son, our Lord, was born of the Virgin Mary. Suffered under Pontius Pilate was crucified, died, and was buried. On the third day, Jesus rose from the dead and is now sitting on the right hand of God the father awaiting to judge the living and the dead.*
>
> *We believe in the communion of saints, the forgiveness of sins, and life everlasting. You and I pray with love and thank God for bringing the two of us together for this miraculous reunion that could only be united in heaven. And I thank God moment by*

moment for the love he has sent to me. I'm in love with you, DiAnnie. You are my girl from The North Country, peace, and grace of the Lord be with you and your mother through Jesus Christ our Lord's name,

Thomas wrote;

Beautiful, how are you doing today, sweetheart? I pray things are going well for you and your mother. I am taking a break and thinking about you continuously, so my mind is passionately in love with you, and the Holy Spirit working through me as let me know that I need to write to you Spiritually.

Although I miss our conversations and miss your sweet voice and speak English so compassionately, your voice is very seductive and precious to my soul. It is music that will bring you, my soul, forever and eternally. Whenever God willing, we get together because we get a karaoke machine to start singing music according to God's will.

I have the spiritual feeling with the feeling of a God-given love that through the Holy Spirit, I will write music that we will both sing together, and it will be precious to a lot of souls out there who need to hear your voice of an angel. You are my girl, and I am in love with you. I pray that is okay with you? Please let me know, sweetheart.

God does not bring two of his children together out of 7 billion without blessing us abundantly. Moses waited in the desert for 40 years before God called on him to set his people free. Moses was 80 years old with a speech impediment, yet he was obedient to God and God's will. Moses was 120 years old when he got called home. God said you could see the promised land, but you cannot set foot on it.

Remember when Moses listened to the people murmur about water, and God told Moses to speak to the rock and bring forth water. Instead of speaking to the rock, Moses was upset and struck the rock with his cane, and the water came forth, not according to what God said, and for that reason, Moses did not get to go into the promised land.

The Bible is a fantastic book of God's will be done immediately or patiently waiting, and we never know what God's plan is for us. This I think we both know as well as your mother is that God loves us unconditionally. And God knows how much I love you.

I'm not sure if you understand or know how much I love you, I have been patiently waiting for this love all of my life, and it is so precious that God showed me. And brought a guardian angel into my life to show me the way to heaven and make me a better man than I am today.

I can only thank you for that, sweetheart, because you are my Northern girl. And your mother is a mighty prayer warrior of who God listens attentively. And for that, I'm thankful.

Then there is a story of Abraham and Sarah, who had their son Isaac when Abraham was approximately 98 years old, and Sarah was approximately 89 years old. Miracles do happen, and we are living testimony to that. I have never known love like I have learned with a beautiful lady such as yourself in my entire life, and for that.

I thank God continuously. You are a great young lady, very beautiful and precious in the eyes of God, and I am proud of you. You're my guardian angel, and I pray to God to always make you happy, never to bring said this to you, if in any way I make you told God will not answer my prayers, this I know because the Bible tells me so.

Paul said this in Galatians, and any man who does not honor or respect and treat his wife with devoted love, God will not hear his prayers. Just let me know that you are happy, sweetheart, because I pray to work out and fast for one day, possibly God willing, that we should meet be together. This I pray through Jesus Christ the Lord's name amen, peace and grace of the Lord be with you and your mother through Jesus Christ our Lord's name amen.

Beautiful, I love how you love me through the grace of God and am in love with you. You are all I think about. I will write you in a few minutes. God bless with love and prayers.

DiAnnie wrote:

Good morning; I hope you had a great night and that you are doing great today, my day started not too long, and I'm about to leave for work. I thought to send a reply to your message and wait to hear from you later. You such a sweet man, honey, and I'm loving you each day. I think both spirits love each other, and having God in it makes us more critical day by day. I thank Him for our lives.

Thanks for always asking how I'm doing. Well, I am doing great, not wanting to complain because of the delays for my trip to The North Country as complaining isn't of the Lord. He wants us to have patient, and the patient is faith, so the two are needed, and that's what I am doing.

I have been busy in recent times with work and running errands. You know, at the ending of the year, things are crazy for a holiday. My day is going well so far, and looking to the rest of the day. Thanks for your concern for my mother and me each time. She asks about you each time we talk and say you are a very good person and praying that she also wants you to make a trip to our house as our guest when she's home from overseas.

I'm going to be the translator because you both wouldn't understand each other..lol.

Anyway, you're in my prayers and heart, and you're the man of life, and trust me, no man can occupy the space you have right now on my hear. God loves you and loves us both.

Peace and hugs and kisses from me.

8 December 2018

DiAnnie wrote;

Hi honey,

I just got back from running some errands this morning and couldn't check my email last night. I was exhausted. Sorry if I didn't get back to you sooner. I hope you had a fair yesterday and today as well.

Thanks for asking how things are going. I will tell you that things are hectic, and I almost feel like a slave, but then one must survive. Life is all about being healthy, so not much to complain about.

I missed you each second that passed. I guess I'll bring joy to people around me and those I meet. For me, in such time, I do share the gospel of Jesus by telling people about why we are celebrating Christmas, trying to reconnect their hearts to Christmas's real purpose.

As I bring in my goods from The North Country and people coming around, I will have the opportunity to share the gospel with them, those I have not met before. I make people smile, so it's another way of bringing joy, so yeah yeah, I'm going to make people happy during the season and wants to make you happy more. My love, you know I'm not a complicated person.

I miss hearing your laughter. It drives me crazy in a positive way. That's a good gift God has blessed you with, honey.

You ask me if you look good as you use to look or me? You never changed to me at all. You're just the same way, almost a year since we met. Here's a recent picture of me, so tell me how I look. Have I changed? lol

I like how you connect the stories of Moses and the Israelites and that of Sarah and Abraham. You and I will be a perfect example of them, but then I am not the same age as Sarah, but there's a connection. Lol, Am I right?

Anyway honey, I am so exhausted now, so I look forward to hearing from you. Enjoy your time, my love.

Hugs and kisses from your Northern treasure.

12 December 2018

DiAnnie wrote;

Good morning my love,

Sorry for my delay. I hope you are having a good day. Mine is going well so far and will get busy soon. I thought to message you since I haven't replied to you since you wrote me.

You make me smile whenever you tell me I'm beautiful because I do not see myself as someone beautiful or proud of myself. It's all must be God, I think.

I will see what I can do. Reading through your message seems like you have traveled quite a while and have experienced different places. Sounds funny how you went to Norway and thought you were eating a hamburger, and it wasn't that. Hunger knows no boundaries, so I just ate, lol.

Ah, you think I can become a singer? Hmmm, maybe a gospel singer because I only want to use my voice for Jesus to praise Him all my life. I think you're a good singer too because I can still remember the other time you left a message on my phone with your songs, believe me, I didn't think it was you till I recognize your voice and said it's Thomas for sure! You sounded like Kenny Rogers to me, lol.

Anyway, how was the course? I have been praying for you concerning that, and in my dream, those people against you seemed happy, and you were unfortunate. My dreams are mostly opposite, but since I dreamed, I haven't felt right, so please tell me what went on. God knows the best.

Well, yes, Mom is okay, and we missed each other, only she thinks I'm still a baby and upsets me sometimes when she thinks I need to be guided in everything, not bad, but you know what I mean, what Moms do..lol.

Honey, I must get running now, so I look forward to hearing from you.

Enjoy the rest of your day—hugs and kisses from Your Girl.

15 December 2018

Thomas wrote:

Beautiful, how are you this evening, sweetheart? Are you angrier than a wet hen? Double smile, I pray you are doing well as can be expected under the circumstances and my homeless apology once again, peace and grace of the Lord be with you and your mother through Jesus Christ our Lord's name amen God bless with love and prayers

What in my message you don't understand?

17 December 2018

DiAnnie wrote:

> *Good morning, my love,*
>
> *I guess you're still in bed. I just woke up and didn't hear from you last night. What happens? Love you and have a good morning.*

18 December 2018

Thomas wrote;

> *Beautiful, you are the funniest little girl I know, and thank you very much for explaining in detail what I. was imagining, now I will not imagine or assuming because now I know big smile with the double grin you're my guardian angel and my sweet precious treasure from The North Country, and I thank you again for explaining your situation, that makes me happy.*
>
> *Big smile with the double grin, and when God joined two people together in the Bible, it had to be miraculous. Communion is a word in the Bible. What do you think communion means, or should I say what does connection mean to you? I love you you are my girl, and you always will be; you are so cute when you get angry, and I do not tell to make you mad I wish I could talk to you on the telephone,*
>
> *I'm a knowledgeable man as well. God would not put two smart people together for no simple reason. God loves us both, and we are going to be together one day, and I certainly do not want to make you feel pressured, that is the last thing on my mind, I was asking questions, I should have started, could you please explain to me in detail why?*
>
> *That may have been a better way to start my conversation with you. Once again, I would never want you to feel pressured. That would be the worst reason to get together with anyone to pressure them, control them, etc. Many men do that to ladies and those of the men I do not care for. I love you. I'm in love with you.*
>
> *I will wait to hear from you, beautiful. You are my girl whether you like it or not smile triple smile with a double backflip, landing on my feet automatically going into a double forward flip stopping in midair to take a rest continuing on the landing next*

to my chair standing up politely setting down and here I am better to get this off to you
I could pinch you on your cheeks you are such a cute double smile.

DiAnnie wrote:

Hello Hun,

Good to hear from you after your silence for a day or two. What happens? Let me clear
some of your doubts here.

Unless you don't want me to go in your heart, I know that's what you're putting God
into it. I know The North Country is away from here, and I have a good reason to go
there.

I have made up my mind, and I don't think I'll let you pressured me. You have done
that too many times, and you always try to do it in another form, is there a reason you
got so many doubts?

You want to go down burning in flames with me? not sure what you mean. I don't
think we are a house divided because I don't see what is supposed to divide us. My heart
is for you, and it has not changed. My feelings for you are positive. I don't want you to
have these negative thoughts about someone you love. This is where the division comes
about if the other person feels sad. No one wants to be pressured, and I'm a lady. Try
to give me some respect, just as I do for you.

That's very good of you, my love, you have a Godly heart, and I appreciate that you
are a blessing to the Texas lady. I think too many crimes in Texas. They have the worse
history of death squads in the US.

I do not ever plan to forget you in my life. If you ever forget me in your life, God himself
will frown on you because I have made you a better man and wants to make you better
as we live in our relationship. I think God has a purpose for our meeting and has a
greater sense for us as we focus on the future. I'm not sure how we both would feel if we
have to be apart. We should never think about this because we have a sweet life ahead.
You're always my Arizonan Zoro, and my earthly hero God is my heavenly hero.

I have to get a few things in order, and I look forward to hearing from you. Enjoy your time till I hear from you—kisses and hugs to you, Mon Amour.

Thomas wrote:

Beautiful,

I'm not sure I understand. Think about this. For the first time Sunday, when Shella with a friend of hers, Jim came down from the Catholic Church and gave me first holy communion, keep in mind the first time.

I'm assuming your trip that you planned on your birthday is not going to happen, and you mentioned your mother was being a mother and possibly not wanting you to go to The North Country. At the same time, she was not there for some reason, and that is only speculation. From what I can read between the lines, your life could be better beautiful. I will pray for you if you pray for me.

I'm saying to myself, are you going to go down and burn flames with DiAnnie? Keep in mind any house divided amongst itself shall not stand. I will wait to hear from you; you will always be my girl I am in love with right now; I am trying to help a lady in Texas who is taking care of her three grandchildren. The parents are all in jail, and I told her to go to some churches. They would be more than happy to help her out. Peace and grace of the Lord be with you and your mother through Jesus Christ our Lord's name amen.

Thomas wrote;

No beautiful I did not mention Arizona. How come you said that word? LOL LOL, you're making me laugh. Let me read the rest of your email. Yes, you have explained your goods to me in The North Country for the third time. I am a man. I'm not real bright, a double smile.

You should know me by now, a triple smile. I'm only a Marine, and please do not get angry; you will make me laugh if you do; that's why I miss our telephone calls. And occasionally, you are hanging up on me for some sick reason. I never laughed so hard.

I say to myself, did DiAnnie hang up on me? I love you, I'm in love with you, and I miss you. I said when the spirit moves you, not when I want you to come. It's going to have to be when the spirit moves you. I'm not a slave driver, LOL. You are so cute.

Thomas wrote;

Beautiful, I mentioned to you before that it is 3750 miles round-trip from The North Country and back, once again explained to me what could ever be that important as far as taking off work? Five thousand eight hundred fifty miles round-trip from Montréal to Phoenix seems to make a little more sense.

Sweetheart, have you thought that if we had gotten together sooner, like 2 Nov, adding on three weeks, you could be pregnant with child. A big smile with a big grin, and us coming together sooner than that.

Through Jesus Christ our Lord, only God knows I do not. You are my precious treasure girl from The North Country with whom I am in love with and always will. And please tell your mother my prayers are with her as well, and my prayers are still with you as you consume my every thought because I love you, and I am in love with you—hugs and kisses from your sweetheart.

Thomas wrote;

My latest picture is taken right now. I cut myself with a razor blade. God said that was for being a bad Zorro.

Thomas wrote;

Beautiful, which is no pressure, so please do not. Feel that I am pressuring you. I should not even mention it to you at this point. I was doing something for a friend of mine, Bob, who I have known since I was 16 years old. And he was in the Navy, and the Navy gave the Marines a ride to hell anytime we needed it. I have been friends for a long time.

I checked on an operation he needs that he does not feel comfortable with the Veterans Administration doing, so I checked on health insurance where Dr. Heinz did my vasectomy reversal. I was checking online at the same time as far as getting your knees medically fixed by the best surgeons in the world that are in Medical Center. When a hospital has valet parking, you know they are catering to the best patients.

Here's the way I perceived that you told me or explain to me that you got into a couple of car accidents, and I'm not exactly in detail what is wrong with your knees? I just wanted to look it up and call there tomorrow or at some point in time to talk to someone about that.

I'm just going to mention that you are my wife. I am a veteran, and that I just had surgery at the Medical Center with Dr. Heinz. And if there's someone I could talk to about my wife, having severe pain in her knees due to an automobile accident.

This is a current picture I had just taken about five minutes ago. I kept my face with a razor, so if you see a little blood trickling down one side of my cheek. You will know that I did not kick myself in the head. I would be rightfully in so doing, double smile. I'm in love with you. It has always been that way from the start.

Do you have an exact date when we started communicating? Or should I say when you started sharing with me? I have 15 Feb 2018, but the email I am looking at from then says that we communicated earlier than that. The best guess I have is about 15 Jan 2018, your birthday, now. Isn't that coincidental, or should I say miraculous? We cannot discard the similarities that we have that I tend to call miracles.

There is more that shall be revealed that we have not even discovered yet. Only in God's time, one by one, remember I am only a man once again for the 50th time. And I would like to think I am a kindhearted Marine who treats his beautiful lady from The North Country like a queen.

You are so precious, and I want to go tie myself up for saying some things that I should not say, and God only knows why, because I sure don't, that hurt your feelings and make you cry I make you feel sad. Every time I think about that, it upsets me and wants to make me cry, I'm so in love with you, and God loves the both of us. This I know because the Bible tells me so. I know you are sleeping. I'm exhausted right now.

I can't keep my mouth off of your double smile with the triple grin. Have a good night, sweetheart. Say your prayers, peace, and grace of the Lord be with you and your mother through Jesus Christ the Lord's name amen.

I'm not sending you any more videos because those videos in my iMac camera are liars, triple smiles. I'm serious because when I look at myself in the restroom at the Hollywood mirror in there. And that mirror will show you a face you have never seen before, and it is so bright. If you're going to look awful, it will be in that mirror. Still, this video camera is the extreme opposite, hard to describe. If you can think of a site where we can both go on and chat from time to time, that would be cool.

I know you are very busy and exhausted almost all of the time, so if you can't or do not care to, that is fine with me. I know what I'm going to do.

My precious sweet girl from The North Country, I'm so in love with you. Anyway, this lady Linda just contacted me out of the blue on Facebook. By the way, can you go on Facebook? Can we instant message there?

I also realize that you are a very busy girl because you are my girl. Anyway, Linda had a brain aneurysm and has had three seizures, lives with her daughter, and has two more operations. And realize that God has a reason for her being here. After praying with her, I explained that I would like to have her story to make others feel good about themselves, and she agreed.

Then my nephew experience the power of God through the earthquake in Anchorage, Alaska. Also, sending me his story and his roommate, who stabbed himself in the stomach and tried to kill himself, went to Tartarus's wrong place. A word that has only been mentioned once in the Bible, usually people go to hell. Tartarus is as far below hell as the earth is below heaven.

I have never heard of anyone coming back from hell, and I'm very interested in writing his story. I might even write a book on that story called "Tartarus" I'm not sure of the title yet. I'm not sure of the title. Others need to have their stories written before they get called home.

It will be a book of miracles and testimonies of others who have gone to heaven and returned. This possibly a book; at some time in the future, I may be writing. And my nephew's minister, believe it or not, is sending me his story as well. When the earthquake hit Anchorage, Alaska, he jumped out of his window a couple of weeks and had the same experience of the only thing we fear is God.

If you know anyone that would like a chapter written in that book that could help others, please do not hesitate to let me know, sweetheart, if it is a story that you feel would be beneficial to others as far as witnessing God in heaven or hell.

I will pray to God that you get back to me. Let me know what you would like me to do? You're so precious and not only in the eyes of God but myself as well. I love you so much, and I am in love with you so much, and God loves both of us.

And if I make you cry one more time or make you feel sad, I'm going to kick myself right in the testicles. And when we get together, I will give you permission first thing to tie me up and whatever you care to do with me.

I would deserve it for being a bad Marine. Marines are only harmful when they are in combat. Marines are supposed to be gentlemen when we are in civilian life, and for me to act like that mostly to my girl was uncalled for and not being a Marine.

Marines are very kind, considerate, and courteous of civilians, and especially Marine's wife? To treat her like that makes me want to cry. I mentioned that I would inevitably, consciously, or unconsciously hurt your feelings because I am a man.

This is no excuse by any stretch of the imagination. You are going to have to tie me up more often than you think, smile double smile. And I will suffer the consequences gratefully and deservedly so with righteous indignation. I love you, honey.

You're my treasure. Solomon said that in the Bible if he could only find one. He was having 700 wives and 300 concubines, the richest man ever recorded in history. The hinges on his horse stables were made of solid gold.

And I have found one treasure, my girl in The North Country, and I make her cry, and you're right; I do not deserve you sometimes. For the things I say to you that are uncalled for, all I can do is thank God for you. That you are so precious and understand and realize that sometimes your Marine is just a jerk, I'm in love with you, and I always have been.

Beautiful, I am angry at myself for making you angry. It does not make me happy that my girl is angry. And I pray to God, for this one, that you tie me up for a long time. I think I'm smiling, and I'm not sure. I am at your beckoning call. What would you like for me to do? After you tie me up and you are satisfied with tying me up, can I give you a big hug and a big kiss?

DiAnnie wrote;

You know how to make me get angry for no reason, you this bad Marine! I always fall into your little trip and contact myself mad at you, which I wouldn't say I like doing because I love you very much, and one thing I wouldn't say I like it whenever I'm trying so hard to make myself clear to someone, and they keep pulling legs makes me wants to die.

Ah, you it's now you ask how I'm doing? Your first message didn't make me feel nice, second too, so for your answer of how I'm doing is I'm so angry at you and wish I had more strength to tie you up, believe when I come over there, I will try to be healthy and whenever you make me angry as you sometimes do.

I'm not going to have petty but will indeed be tied you hard indoor till you promise me not to anger me. I was not a skinny girl to treat you like a marine too.

I'm not praying for them to be silly, though. I have been busy today running errands. You're so funny, Thomas. You make me laugh though I am angry. Bible sure does not have emails and telephones. All was natural! I only know communion being to remember the flesh and blood of Christ. Do you have any other meaning of connection?

Love you.

Thomas wrote;

Thank you, thank you beautiful, you know how much I love you, and you know me I am mad at myself I am going to kick myself right in the groin, I'm so in love with you.

22 December 2018

DiAnnie wrote;

> *Good morning hun,*
>
> *I have gotten your latest messages, and believe me, I haven't been in the mood to write, plus being busy as well. I hate to hide my heart from someone I love, so it is better to say what is going on inside my heart to you.*
>
> *Since we met, it has been almost a year, and if you also think right about me, you'll realize that I am an understanding person and one that does not push you against the wall. It's not like I am not making an effort to work; I do just that the needs of a woman are huge, and you as a man should know that and also, in a relationship, you do not expect a lady to ask her man about her needs so don't try to make it like I am making you go through hell.*
>
> *You're very good at misunderstanding me; it's not compulsory that I must have a man before I can survive, I have survived without a man, and you know even as we met, you have not been supporting me each month I am still staying.*
>
> *I have God, and He cares more than anyone above and below this earth when I say you're not the man for me. I mean, you're someone that does not hold back harsh words towards a lady you suppose to love.*
>
> *Words hurt more the even physically assault, and that's my problem. I appreciate God because I have work and healthy alive, and I can get medication when I have my knees pain.*
>
> *So I'm not looking for a man to get a better life and respect and true love, a man who would honor his lady and respect her. You know, no matter what you and I say to each other, one thing I never keep from you is respect.*
>
> *I respect you a lot and will always do no matter how harsh you're too towards me. I listen to my Mom and God the last. You're not worthless at all to me, you're a great guy Thomas, and I wouldn't deny that, but you have a clever way of saying bad things. And only a person who is not intelligent wouldn't know. I appreciate you in many ways, you have helped me, and I don't deny it. I hope you understand.*

I was also frustrated like I say and felt let down, but it's all part of life, and I will not hate you for that. I hope you understand and believe me if I am ever in the position. I will be glad to help you. I'm hoping that all those things my Mom and I are running after will work out, and those monies that belong to my Dad will get to us.

I genuinely love you, and you make me feel good, especially your sense of humor. These are good things a lady wants in a man, not bad, harsh words.

I never intend to make you sad, so don't get me wrong. You are not a liar, and I would never say that to you when I get angry or anyone for that reason. Nothing positive comes from an angry person. My aunt used to tell me that when someone is mad at someone, the one mad at shouldn't expect nice words or sweet praises from the one angry, because that's what it is called Anger!

So I'm sorry I made you feel bad, and I want a sorry from you too for saying bad words cleverly. I know it's impossible to go our separate ways because we are just the perfect couple, and disagreements are meant in any relationship. A relationship with no ups and down is never enjoyable, and it is such as ours that we will sit tomorrow and realize where we came from. You are that old Zoro that says terrible things!

I realize the issue has had a lot on you; you have no choice but to continue to pray to the Lord for a solution. I know it's just a matter of time things will change for us. Pray that the issue that Mom traveled there will have some positive news soon. My Mom wants me to travel to her as quickly as possible.

So I only extended your regards as usual to her and said she hope you're doing well.

Sounds good on your new project about putting stories together about people. Did your nephew Samuel's report include? I think you remember talking about him and another lady from Texas. I hope I am right. I will try to see if I get some interesting stories I can send you to add to the project. I am becoming a good writer because of you. I have never written to anyone as I have done to you.

I think our two spirits agree so much, and I see us going a long way in this life and heaven. Our main reasons as Christian are to save a soul or, say, bringing a soul to the kingdom of God.

Hey honey, you wrote a nice story there, and I was following, and you think I will be bored?

No, I enjoyed reading, and all rested on Brian's head again lol you and Brian will get me to go mad laughing when I read about you two. You guys would be great entertainers for me when I come over there to live. I am smiling as I read, lol. You're a great writer, and I wish the ages of those ancient people were still possible in our times to reach 120 years and even 500 years, lol. If my Zoro can be around reaching 500 years would be nice, I will maybe be able to tie you up for 100 years to change from saying bad things cleverly.

Thanks for your messages and all the encouragement. You just know how to make a lady love you so much. Please, let's try not to hurt one another again. Enjoy your day, and I look forward to hearing from you.

Much love from me as usual, and hey, nothing has changed. I'm still your big fan! Hugs and kisses. Your Northern queen.

Thomas wrote;

You're not going to believe this, and don't smile, please, LOL. I just wrote this extensive email to you took me about one hour. I accidentally hit delete.

Thomas wrote:

Beautiful, and you know what happened, it went goodbye; I feel that it is the small penance I have to pay and try to redo this again. It was so long my photographic memory could not even begin to pour out the feelings I was writing for you.

So here we go again. I know you're laughing; this is no laughing matter, double smile with a big grin, you are bubblegum to my eyes. Where was I before I so mistakenly threw my email in mid-air to you? Anyway, I'm glad you wrote me an email with the extensive link you usually do. How are you doing?

And what have you been doing? How is your mother doing? I pray everything is going well for you and your mother, and thank you for letting me know to keep praying for you as I always do anyway and I thank you for your prayers.

I'm in love with you, and I love you, and you and I both know that money cannot buy the love we have. Our passion goes beyond that. It is spiritual and holy, and it came from God. You and I have too many things in common to have just been coincidental. God put us together, and we fit like a hand in the glove. This is what I feel.

I also realize that I hurt your feelings to make you angry. I'm not making this an excuse, being married, having lady friends in Alcoholics Anonymous, and friends throughout the 16 years or better. God has so patiently answered our prayers for one another and that we belong to one another through the grace of God.

There is no other reason that I can think of other than God's grace, which is why we got together. To dishonor God by not praying, respecting, and thanking God extensively for our relationship of which we have been communicating.

I should say just under a year. I'm going to send you a picture of Brian. He is 61 years old, by the way, looks and walks like it's 161 years old, smile the picture is of Brian myself and the Catholic nun who came and stayed with us.

I said to Brian, run you through the brush chipper, directly into the septic tank, let you decompose for about six months. have the septic tank truck come up and pump your remains, and take you to the San Francisco sewage plant, where they will give you a friendly burial at sea. Double smile with the backflip, LOL.

I'm proud of you, you're a great lady, and you are my girl, sweetheart. I am working hard and thinking up every way I can through prayers, praying for an abundance of blessings that will bring us together instead of keeping us apart.

Anyway, back to why I am so misunderstood and harsh and mean to a guardian angel God has given to me. Treating her with disrespect and not understanding your lifestyle precisely. I know we communicate, and you let me know exactly what is going on.

And for that, I appreciate your love for me. I am so proud of you and your great woman, and I do not know what I would do without you in my life. And God knows that there is something spiritually I feel that we both have to go through, and I'm not sure exactly what it is.

That's why I said I don't know because I don't. I do not know the mind of God, but I do know that he loves his children. And he loves you and me when we give him respect and love through our prayers and knowing Jesus Christ our Lord and Savior. And once again, can you please forgive me for not understanding the excuses? I do understand, and the circumstances are severe.

There's nothing I can do about it right now, right this moment. God has something good in mind for us. I have experienced too many miracles in my life of biblical proportions to know any different, and my faith is unshakable. My nephew Samuel and his roommate, and his minister send me their stories in the mail, and thank you.

Please try to collect miraculous stories that you may happen to run across so I can put this book together. Everybody asked me to pray for them. They know I am a prayer warrior, and I pray to God. I know he does know that I am praying for these people to pray for them, and I'm not God. God answers prayers through the Holy Spirit when they are meant to be answered, and not one second before or after; I do know that.

Sometimes, patients are a miraculous answer to someone's prayer, and the only thing is we want everything right now, right this minute. DiAnnie, please believe me when I tell you this, the end times are right here; I have a spiritual feeling we will be caught up in heaven and will not have to stay here seven years for the tribulation.

According to Revelation, Daniel's book, and all the prophets, seven years of pure hell. I'm just asking God nicely, and this you might pray for us as well. Very kindly and lovingly with compassion for God and Jesus Christ, that we may have the opportunity to meet one day. This life that God has so graciously written in the book of life.

Am I getting this off to you before I lose it? My other one was longer than this one can you believe it? Don't laugh. I know you are laughing. You think this is funny, don't you? Now that I'm at the end of this letter, I can laugh at myself. It was not funny when I hit the delete key accidentally. Peace and grace of the Lord be with you and your mother through Jesus Christ the Lord's name.

You are my precious guardian angel treasure girl from The North Country, and I am your Zoro. God bless, I love you, and I will write another letter. There are some things in the first one that, unfortunately, as you can see, I could not memorize that letter word for word. have you ever thought that when you're in survival mode that you do not have time to dream?

Thomas wrote;

Beautiful Guardian Angel, now take a look at this, if this is the world between God's love, God's love, God's love. Now we both know how much God loves us, or at least we think we do; smiles, love for us are eternal and never-ending. So ours is infinite and never-ending as well.

I was listening to a minister very well-known and renowned, and there are some things I disagree with him.' number one, he says there is never a perfect marriage that did not ring true within my soul. Getting to know each other over this last past year, we have had our ups and downs.

And I thank God, for the most part, they were on paper, and I have the unshakable faith that when we do finally meet. It will just be our spirits and souls that come together, not our minds or our love for one another because all we have is our love through God and the Holy Spirit to guide us through this life helping other people—either observing our love for one another or us to reach out and help others. Our passion is boundless progressive, and eternal with compassion. I feel my heart there will never be a harsh word between us.

Until I can get right with God and myself, in my heart and the soul, that has been holding me back. Then I say to God, and I do not say anything to God I humbly ask God. God, please help me. I don't know what to do, and I need help through the Holy Spirit to become one of your children. So I can have a divine love for my girl DiAnnie, a guardian angel you put into my life.

She is all good and has brought nothing but blessings to my life, and for that, I thank you, God. I am proud of her. She has made me the man I am today and walking across time throughout the last year. I have steadily, because of this guardian angel, made progress in a significant way, and God, you and I both know that.

I love this Guardian Angel that you put into my life. I realize I do not deserve her at this point. I feel that she is my guardian angel and knows it in my heart because she loves me. And she has the courage, strength, and wisdom to hang onto this worthless soul. I want to feel that love of God, and I want to do all the right things in my life.

The truth is like an onion that you have to peel layer by layer until you get to the core. That's why reading the word of God from the Bible strengthens my spiritual discernment and knowing right from wrong. Then I take a look at the inside of my heart and soul—the personal side, not the side that helps others because that's endless.

I have to be honest, caring, loving patiently waiting for God to do the right thing in my life. Once again, I ask God daily, God, please help me, through Jesus Christ the Lord's name, to be a better man. I feel I have to start learning to love myself and feel and know that.

I am a good man, and because of you, DiAnnie, only this could be possible. You're changing me from within the inside, and on the surface, anyone can look good. I'm finding out the more of the Bible I read, of God and Jesus Christ and the Holy Spirit.

DiAnnie, I have passed skeletons in my closet, and I have to do some closet cleaning, for the simple reason I think to myself if I was to get an overabundance, all of a sudden. It would be like the Garden of Eden and Satan tempting Eve to take the forbidden fruit.

My priority is my guardian angel, you are so precious, and I'm so proud of you. How are you feeling today, sweetheart? Are your knees bothering you?

I want to prove to you that nothing is impossible, sweetheart, if I can live out my dream. I'm not sure if you know how much I love you. I want to provide you with a home in a safe environment that can live out your dreams. There is a light, a certain kind of light that is—never shown on me until I met you.

Baby, you do not know what it's like to love somebody the way there love you. It's like that dream I was explaining to you at one point in time, not sure if you remembered. All the plans that I dream of, including our love for one another, disappears into thin air just before about ready to receive it. I have never known the love that I feel for you. This is why I know it is from God.

You know what I think about and still, make me laugh? Is when you said, "do not pull my legs," the proper phrase is, "do not pull my leg." I have never heard anyone pulled two legs on somebody. Until you said it, and I'm not kidding, you made me laugh, and I still laugh thinking about that. This is why I love your voice. It is the voice of an angel, and you speak English very well. It is just every once in a while. You might come up with the phrase that is not American.

And your sense of humor in that respect makes me. I want to love you more. And we are going to sing music together. I have the spiritual feeling that your voice with my voice will be like a song from the Angels. And it will most certainly be a song that we have written together that we have written, and it will be a spiritual song about God.

Ensure you let your mother know that my prayers are with her, thinking about her safety, and praying for her trip. Piece of the grace of the Lord be with you and your mother through Jesus Christ the Lord's name amen I'm in love with you, and I love you.

How could I not? You were sent from heaven, you are a great woman DiAnnie, and once again, I would not be the man I am today, or if it were not for our little dispute that made me do some soul-searching, because I had no real answers for the way I was talking to you. And I had to look at myself, and I'm changing more and more for good through your spiritual discernment.

And we both do not realize it because it is from God and the Holy Spirit; this is how we grow; if we think it's about us, we are in big trouble. So let us give thanks and praise to God for connecting two powerful children of God that will manifest and spark a lot of the love into people we love you, I love you, I love you.

23 December 2018

DiAnnie wrote;

Hello Sweet man, How is Mr.?

It's a pleasure hearing from you once again, I was looking forward to your last message before replying, and I just got it. It is frustrating when you put in your time to write something nice, and mistakenly it gets deleted by yourself, so I know how it feels..lol, but no worries, I still appreciate the fact that I hear from you each time you. How is your day going? Guess you guys are preparing for Christmas.

I'm doing the same as well. I'll spend Christmas day with a few people from church. Mom is also planning to visit a nearby church there as it is important to be in the presence of the Lord. Thanks for asking. I'm doing great, just that what I expected didn't materialize, but I must accept it the way it is. Not much has been going on here recently apart from work. I had to reapply because I told my boss I would be away for a few days. So I only have three days off and will be busy again.

Good, you realize that a lady needs security, especially someone who wants to help themselves and help their family. I know in years to come, I'll be the one to work for us, you're no more working, and in time your age will increase as mine will but not at the same pace.

So I would be much stronger to also care for you. For me, I look beyond life, not just for now. I won't have thought this way if I do not have a future with you in my heart. I wouldn't care to think about the long run. I prefer someone being a witness to my character to blowing my own trumpet. So good that you can see the difference between the ladies you have had in your life and me and the ones you have met.

I would never want to sleep with a person I know deep in my heart I don't love. That's the last thing I would ever want to do. If I didn't love you, I don't think I'll be here till now or you as well, because true love does not come from ourselves because human nature looks mostly at SELF which makes it impossible to love another from a Godly viewpoint.

Not many young girls would like an older man and one with a disability. I don't look at that because God made me love you just as you are. I see you as you, I'm a young person, and the feeling of loving someone according to my SELF imagination is there. Still, it is not always right because what my heart wants isn't what God wants.

It is better to leave my SELF, which is my enemy, to follow God for me and not against me. I hope you get the point I'm trying to explain to you. So my love for you is genuine and not from man but God. We have too many things in common because God knew He needed like-minded persons to love and be a blessing to His kingdom.

I know you have hurt me many times, but if I do decide to keep things in my heart, then I do not have a forgiving heart, and such attitude isn't of God, so I always have a big room in my heart to forgive you because I love you truly.

That is an excellent picture of you, Brian, and the nun. You're so funny. Brian is 61 but walks like he's 161? hahaha, good he knows about me. I don't see why it should be a threat to him because there's nothing to hide here and nothing to think he can say out there; I do not owe anyone anything.

We love each other. That's the fact, and God made it possible. You are right, though, to warn him because, as men, it's not good running your mouth around. I guessed when you told Brian what was going to happen to him. Did he get a real scare, right? No one wants to die, lol. No worries, well, he saw my nice pics, and what did he say about them?

You have been forgiving Zoro. As I said, I will always forgive you because I do not know how to hate someone I love. I will send you any exciting stories as soon as I come across any for your book, okay? I see the end time is real, and it's only those who are lost who should be worry and I'm sorry about them too because they have chosen not to understand the reality around us that is going on around the world, according to the book of Revelations.

According to that preacher, it is only true to the ordinary person if there is no true or perfect marriage. Still, those in the Lord know true and ideal marriage do exist when God is in it.

So a marriage that is not perfect must not have God's approval. Yes, ours is God's, and no matter our shortcomings, we still stand up again, which to me is because God wants it to survive and be a testimony to people and be a blessing to people.

I have fought hard in my life to have things I want, to be the girl I am physical, being attractive and beautiful isn't overnight, if I didn't look clean, beautiful, and control my structure, I don't think you would even consider exchanging messages till now, even if you disagree.

Deep in your heart, you are not looking for a girl that isn't clean and classic. So if a girl is asking her man to help her stay clean as she has been. I don't think a man who wants his girl in good shape to complain. I'm just expressing myself as a lady, and you have to understand. I'm not saying you are not my type. You are a clean person, and I like you for that, so when I say I need this or that it's not for pleasure but to stay in good shape.

A lady has many needs, and some ladies put all their burdens on their men. I am not like that. I have things I want to do to earn money and not burden my man for everything. Let me tell you one thing my Mom and I have been undertaking, we have purchased many things, from accessories to clothes, foodstuff and name it that we want to have on a ship to Sicily or somewhere for that matter to sell and have enough to live on, we have proposed this. When the Lord answers us soon, we will have a container with those items.

I think you are honest with yourself, and I do admire that from you, you are someone that wants to change, and you need a helper. I am here to help you change whatever keeps holding you back. I may not know about you, which I would be glad to know and help you change.

We have a huge future ahead, and I need to know everything as my husband to be. I know there must be a reason that you don't provide for me as you should. I'm not so worried about that. I worry about you, our kid's future, and how life will be when we start to live together.

I do not want to pack out tomorrow, and people ask what happen to your marriage.

I look beyond and think deeply. These are things I must be sure of before coming over to you. Believe my mind is made up, and I know I am yours. I know you care for me and I too care and worry about you the most because I ask myself each time, how is my Zoro doing?

Has he eaten today? What are the things he's struggling with? I may sound like I don't seem to care sometimes but believe me, I think about you so much, just as you do for me. You are also my priority. I feel good, my love and my knees are behaving recently. I wish they would stay this way forever. Lol.

Honey, you don't have to stress to prove to me if you love me or not. I know you genuinely do. Any man that says sorry when there's a fight is honest, and the same with a lady. We are not so big to say we are sorry each time, so yes, I know you love me truly, and there are no doubts in my heart that you do love me.

I also ask myself the same questions if you believe I love you? I know you do, and I know my own heart, but your heart, my Zoro, do you feel deep within your heart that this young girl loves you? Truly? If your answer is yes, I will be the happiest girl in the world! Which means I have the assurance that we are on the same path.

Well, not everything that goes on between us. I have to tell people or even my Mom. There should be secrets between the two of us. If I told my Mom, she would have said something negative, like, better you leave Thomas if he treats you this way.

She likes you, but you know she will not like you more than her kid, she's not the wrong person, but that is natural to love your own. She loves you for the fact that you love me and not going ever to hurt me.

Hahaha, thanks for the correction, don't pull my legs, please!!! Lol, pull my leg. I know I only hear this in English but have not written it before, so since humans have two legs, I thought it was right to say don't pull my legs, not knowing it was just an Idiomatic expression.

You're a good teacher and never hesitate to correct me when I fall short in English, yes true I'm good but not perfect and glad we can have a language to communicate with if I didn't pay much attention to the English language in school how possible would it be communicating with an Arizonan? Impossible right? Thanks to my English teachers and stay some time in English Anglophone The North Country. I miss your voice too, and hopefully, soon I will have a phone. Hey, it's not like I can't have a telephone, okay I will laugh so much the day we are recording our music. I will be Celine Dion and you Kenny Rogers. Lol.

Not sure if you read what I told you in my last message. Mom wants me to travel to her soon. I believe it would be in a hurry, so it better I let you know before time, so I'm getting my things ready. I did call already for my passport, and it will be prepared this week. Mom is arranging for my ticket, so if it is possible to stop over to you, we will see. If not, we can make a stopover upon our return, or better, we get home and visit you. I'll give you updates on that.

I'm getting tired now so I'll stop here for now and I will look forward to hearing from you. Thanks so much for staying in touch. My endless love, my best friend, the guy I fight with and we make peace, lastly my Zoro lol.. it is Christmas eve tomorrow, what're your plans? I don't know why I love you so so so much! Kisses and hugs.

28 December 2018

DiAnnie wrote;

> *Good morning my love,*
>
> *Sorry, it has been a few days since you heard from me. First, I wish you a Merry Christmas! Sorry for my delay. I didn't think it was going to take me a few days to get back to you. I went to Laval to spend Christmas with a friend from church, the invitation came unexpected, it was to be until New Year, but I needed to be home to put a few things together, she wasn't feeling so well but is trying now.*
>
> *How have you been keeping? I hope you had a lovely Christmas with your family and Brian. Give me news on how it went. I'm eager to hear about it.*
>
> *Awee...your sweet words have me drawn to you too! I am reading all the messages you sent me recently from scratch, making me feel so happy. You're a nice man Thomas, and I never regretted ever meeting you and having you in my life. I appreciate all these lovely and romantic words; you know how to have a lady drawn to you.*
>
> *You're one in a kind among millions of men, and I was so amazed at how God directed our paths. You're not just a kind-hearted person but also a man full of humor and romance, you're protective in many ways, that's all a lady needs, and you have all these qualities which I so appreciate very much.*
>
> *Thanks for being so honest to tell me about your life. I knew you have had a bad past and have experienced negative relationships. Though you are changing for the better, there are still some more changes needed, which I will address in response to your last recent message. So I'll come to that later, back to what I was saying.*
>
> *I know you love me, and I do appreciate every moment we share in our lives. I like you to know that when I say I love someone, it's not just to say it, but it comes from deep within me. So I will always hold you by your words, all that you speak to me, so whenever you try to be different towards me in a negative way and forgetting all you have said, then I may think you are just saying these things from your lips, not from your heart.*
>
> *So be real, and I hold you by your words that there is no law, reason, or idea holding you back your secure love for me.*

This, to me, isn't a mere saying. It's something I hold dear to my heart and makes me love you more.

Well, love hurts in many ways. It can hurt positively and negatively. For us, we are overcoming the negative part of our love life and getting more positive, so honey, you shouldn't be hurt because nothing is going to change me from loving you no matter what.

The love we share is beyond human comprehension, and it's only the both of us truly understand. If we were not meant to be, I don't think we would have survived all the fights we have had. It's because God planned this before we know it, and we can only bear witness as we see in our lives.

You're right. We are meant to be. I see this because the love we share is only through God's eyes we can realize that we are blessed. I appreciate you very much. The love you have for me, the care, and understanding will always have me drawn to you, and I promise to love you, care for you as well, respect you till the end.

Well, I too wish we met longer, but we do not control time. It's only God, so He allowed His timing, and who are we to question it? So we just flow according to His time. We are having a good relationship because He is in it! So I have no regret why we didn't meet sooner.

No matter the time in life, it is the excellent relationship between two people that matters, so I am focused on having a good relationship with you full of love, compassion, caring, romance, and God's word being the center of it all.

Wow, I appreciate how you connected the word of God and believe it's just the truth. It's all centered around God's timing. Thanks very much, my love. You are a great writer, and I connect so quickly when I follow along.

I like it when you say Mr. lol it goes so well with it..lol I do not realize that I write much when I'm writing to you. I feel like I'm right before you talking because it is very difficult ignoring every piece that you write to me.

After all, I find everything interesting because I love you very much, so I do not realize I have written many books! I am this excellent writer now because of you because you're not boring at all. I feel so happy for the degree of respect and love you have for my

Mother. She respects you and thinks you're the best person for me because I translated some of your messages into French and sent it to her.

So she knows you so well more than you think..lol, well my Mom is overprotective. It left with me to let her know the type of character you're, so she's getting a better picture of you these days, remember she didn't know you when she told me to be respectful to you, she's a nice person but also wants the best for her daughter so reason she's overprotective.

Hahaha...Brian is scare of his boss. I guess he knows what you capable of doing. Well, you never know, what has he done in his life? Yes, I meant what I said that I don't care anymore about how anyone would feel about you and me, you're my Zoro, and no one can ever change it.

Thanks for understanding. I get busy sometimes that I feel almost like a slave. Good; you have been there and understand when someone is busy, so sometimes I know it's never intentional when I do not message sooner.

You have more time than me. It's just the reality. I know from some of your messages you sound as if I forget you, never that, Sir. You are always on my mind, and not a day that goes by that you are not in my heart. I do think of how you go day by day, what life is like for you. I hope I'm not overprotective over you like my Mom does..lol.

I will send you an address to receive your latest book. I think I have received this book before. I will check the title of the ones I have, candies? Lol, that would be cool. Well, pieces of jewelry aren't bad. I don't mind if they are expensive or not.

It's the intentions of the person buying a piece of jewelry for their lover that matters. Pieces of jewelry have deep meanings, even in ancient times. I got a lot of jewelry, though, so I wouldn't want too much unless they are very important. I'm still waiting to hear from my Mom about my trip, so I will let you know about it as soon as I know anything.

I let go of my own needs and have you settle yours. After all, you have needs as well, and I do care for you as well. If things well going as I plan, believe me, I would have helped you as much as I can, I know soon things will get better, and I will be able to help you too. Sad that the rest of your family is doing this to you just because you stand for the truth. That's how the upright suffers in the hands of the unrighteous.

That's how the world has been to this day. I think God made it that way always to expose those who are not upright to leave their wicked ways, but I think instead of your family realizing it's an opportunity for them.

Thanks always for your prayers for us. That's so important, good I have a prayer warrior such as you, my love, all power last in God's hands, and having a prayerful husband is the best. I am, too, and do pray for you each time.

I am so proud of you, my Zoro, that you wrote such a sweet message. I feel so bad that I could not write you on Christmas Day, you know too many things have come in the way, especially during this time. Thanks for remembering me, honey, and I love you so much.

DiAnnie wrote:

Now I will get to your latest message, which made me feel bad a bit. Honey, I realize that not hearing from me for a few days has already changed you, and I know your last message was not intentional. I know you so very well, first. Do you think I am pressuring you for you to take care of me? If I did ask you in my last message why do you love me, I didn't mean to hear such a message from you about me having to find a man that can take care of me.

I told you in my message why I love you, so instead of giving me such a cold message, I rather wanted to hear a different thing, not a negative thought, but that's you, whenever you don't hear from me, you start to behave in the other way, I am not going to worry about that since I know you already. If you are honest with me, I am one person that does understand you very much and does not push you against the wall for anything, but sometimes I wonder why you say certain things to me, you think when I do not call or write it means I am with another man?

I am not like that; I feel sad when you try to think that way about me.

All God wants to change for bringing me into your life. He wants us to share much to make you the man you have never thought of being. We are similar in many ways and love each other. Why do you think I will change or leave you out of my life so quickly? is trust still the issue with you?

Do you think you are not a man enough for me? If yes, why do you think that way? Is there a problem that you are always pushing me for a way to find another man? If you trust me and love me, you will have confidence in me and not think I am cheap or looking for a person to care for me.

I try my best to care for myself, so stop saying all these sad things. Reading all your messages made me feel so happy until reading the last one. Please tell me why you wrote the previous message. What was going on in your heart? Please be honest, my love.

I look forward to hearing from you. I wish you a great day. Know that I will never love anyone else as long you continue to love me. Enjoy the rest of your day till I hear from you.

You are always my Zoro. Kisses and hugs.

Thomas wrote;

My sweet, beautiful Guardian Angel, Whom I am in love with, is from The North Country, and she is precious in God's eyes and for my salvation. Sweetheart, when I do not hear from you, I realize that you are busy, and I am proud of you, is everything going okay in your life? Are you feeling okay? What have you been doing for excitement, smiled?

I'm in love with you, we have written volumes and many books together you and me I. Realizing also that your life is busy and do not have the time that I have to write to you, and I have learned not to let my imagination go wild when I do not hear from you okay? Knowing that we love one another with a deep heartfelt emotion that will never end, for the simple reason it was given to us by the grace of God.

Amazing grace "a gift freely given of God" such as our love, the song Amazing Grace, was written by John Newton, a slave trader that brought African-Americans from Africa to the United States, and the African-Americans were treated with cruelty beyond the imagination and Newton certainly was of that character, when he turned his life around and got saved, he remembers that tune that came from the bowels of the ship that the slaves were chanting and singing. He then put his pen to parchment and wrote Amazing Grace's words for those tunes he had heard from those slaves. Now here is something that may be of interest to you, you complete every tune and word to that song on the piano only on the black keys. That song was born out of slavery and through the grace of God.

Christmas eve, the day before Christmas, I was lying on my bed watching and listening to my favorite biblical evangelist. When the telephone rang, it was a lady that I met in the program many years ago. The last time I had seen her, I was supposed to go to church with her at a Baptist Church.

I was so burnt out I should say I was so satisfied with writing to you just about all night long that she came to pick me up. I refused and explained to her that I was writing most of the night to you, and she got so upset with me that she cussed me out with every cuss word you could imagine, and I had never seen her for about six months. Now maybe?

Back on Christmas Eve, I was a witness and a testimony to why I have one arm that was an answer to my prayer at the time where I would not be here right now. Still, being mean unconsciously, God put me in a wheelchair that I am getting out of slowly and learning to be a kind-hearted person thanks to you. The minister at the church could not believe that losing my arm was an answer to my prayer and why I was not angry at God? I said I accepted at the moment it happened and could not have thought of it as being any other way than in answer to my prayer. Because it took me off Harley's motorcycles, I was riding with an evil group from Arizona and was just going to get another Harley and go back to riding with that group.

I kept up with the testimonies of miracles that had happened in my life, like when my brother got called home going to an Alcoholics Anonymous meeting on his Harley and getting hit by a deer that killed him instantly. And not five minutes before he was sitting in my bedroom and we were talking, and how he came to me the next morning, opened the door and cooked breakfast like he usually did at my home and talk to the cat Arnold that he tamed.

I did not say a word when I smell the bacon and heard him talk to the cat because I knew it was only his spirit. Then, the gentleman staying in the shack where Brian is staying now came into my house and said, I don't know if I hear things or go crazy. He proceeded to say that my brother just opened his door and slammed it, and told him to get up. Then another friend of mine lost his cell phone, and my brother came to him in a dream that night and told him what was at.

Then at the service, I also witnessed a time it was 3 a.m. The Holy Spirit woke me up for some religious reason, and it was a warm summer night. I went out and sat on the front porch in my underwear, and I saw a young girl run down the driveway and went and hid behind one of my work trucks. Right behind her was some Mexican-American guy chasing after her in his car. She asked me if I saw Teresa, funny I still remember her name. I thought it was just the teen girls who lived in the trailer next door to me who got into a fight with her boyfriend, and I told him to get off the property, or I was going to get my gun and blow him away.

He looked at me and took off as fast as he could. The next morning, the Mother came over who had two beautiful teenage girls in high school, and the girl Teresa that ran down my driveway was one of the girls' friends. It turned out this guy for two days had been raping her and abusing her, and she just had the opportunity to get out in front. The Mother said that was the real deal, and I shared that I want to share about you and me at the service, and there will come a time when we will be a witness to many others, and we can share our story. Because it is a miraculous story, and God wants us to tell it through the Holy Spirit of truth honesty with holy grace.

I brought this lady to her home, picked her up the next day to spend Christmas with us, and took her back home. She has a Christian, and she was praying. She did not know what she was going to eat because she was hungry or how she would get her car out of being impounded, or where she was going to spend Christmas. God works in mysterious ways. Anyway, the Holy Spirit working through me witness to about 25 people and a Baptist Church minister. And if anyone of them did not believe in God or Jesus Christ or the Holy Spirit, most certainly when I got finished witnessing for God Jesus Christ and the Holy Spirit, they did then. I have so much more to write, but I will wait to hear from you, beautiful you're my girl; I am proud of you, your precious and the love of my life. Peace and grace of the Lord be with you and your Mother through Jesus Christ the Lord's name amen.

Postscript. I have many more miracles that have happened throughout my life. You and I. are the biggest miracle that is ever happened in my life. This love we have for one another has come through God's grace. I cannot pray for this love because it was God's grace. I love you so much.

Thomas wrote;

My beautiful treasure of a guardian angel. I realize more and more how strong our love is for one another, and as I had mentioned before, I need to be hit on the head a few times before I. finally get it, smile, and that's why I thank God for you and why I am so proud of you because you teach me that can only come from a godly woman, and equally yoked spiritually is our priority through the grace of God.

And I'm not sure if I would agree with you on all the fights we have had, double smile with a big grin, I find that it is a good thing that we have had a few disagreements with one another that only made us stronger in our love for each other. Would you not agree? And I certainly not intending on fighting continuously or arguing to make our love stronger, that would be silly, and I feel we know each other well. Our love for one another is from the Holy Spirit and is so powerful and beyond our comprehension.

I pray you can understand what I am saying, you're so beautiful and precious, and I have never regretted our love from day one because I knew my heart of hearts that you are my girl, I just had to question God at first for this love sent me, that is when I need to get knocked on the head a few times by you, double smile with the big grin, I'm so in love with you, and it has been that way from the very start as I. have said before. I need to keep reminding myself of that. And it hurts my heart to know that I make you feel sad, so I will try not to do that anymore. You love me, and I know this in my heart, and you know that I love you in your heart, and from 7 billion people, you are my girl and so precious in the eyes of God.

No amount could by our love for one another, and together one day, we will experience a love neither of us has ever known. And it will continue to grow of all the ocean so deep and from the sky to sky is the endless and eternal love of God that much I know between you and me. There will never be a harsh word between us, only helping others to witness our love together.

I realize you and your Mother have many things to do in your lives, and I would do nothing to interfere with that. Those are certainly not my intentions. I want you to feel free in our love for one another and know that when I do not hear from you for a while, it is for a perfect reason, and you are a busy lady, a wonderful busy lady.

And I continuously pray for you and your Mother, understanding your Mother's love for you and certainly wanting the best for you since all you have known of each other is family for one another. And all of a sudden, this Marine comes along a big smile with a double grin. I feel that God answered our prayers either consciously or unconsciously, and I think your Mother will realize this as time goes by. I'm in love with you, also acknowledging that your Mother and yourself are the only family you have known and that I am a part of your family for eternity.

So you're not alone. Let your Mother know with confidence and appreciation that I am just not another guy. I am precious in the eyes of God for a reason there's only one of me in 7 billion. There has been a time when we have not been, and now there is a time we will always be, either 1 billion years from now or 1 trillion years from now, we will always be.

Sweetheart, we only come this way once, we went into this world with nothing, and we live the same way; it's what we do in the eyes of God that will make the eternal difference for our love for one another. And you know what to do if I hurt your feelings or make you feel sad, hit me on the head, double smile with a big grin, what you have been doing all along. And you do not realize how many times I kick myself in the pants for saying some of the things I have told you. It is not easy to kick myself in the pants, LOL. That would feel much better than the way I feel in my heart when I make you feel sad.

I will write you another email until I hear from you before I lose this one and kick myself in the pants again; double smile with the triple grin arguing with my wife is like trying to blow out a lightbulb. A smile I'm in love with you, precious.

I just had two ladies recently say to me, "don't you ever get older?" And I met a minister who was one year younger than I am, who looked like he was 168 years old, so here we are and where we will be together one day. A young couple in love, peace, and grace of the Lord be with you and your Mother to Jesus Christ our Lord's name amen double hugs and triple kisses

Thomas wrote;

My beautiful Guardian Angel of God, if you do not think money is necessary, try to take a $100 bill from the person standing next to you, we will have the world vast wrestling arena right here right now if you try it, smile remember no worry no stress and everything is okay right this very moment does not go five minutes ahead in your *mind or five minutes behind you that is over and done worth, right this very moment as you are reading this everything is okay.*

Once again, one moment of worry, stress, or negativity is a moment of happiness you will never get back. There is an endorphin released according to medical science in our bodies if we have joy and laughter, it keeps us from getting older faster, so be happy, joyous, and free, release those endorphins within your body that will keep you young for a long time as I have learned to do, I am happy 24 seven except in a moment when my beautiful treasure girl from candidate is sad, then for that moment I am not excited, I am so low I cannot even pay attention, a smile I'm as poor as a church mouse, smile and if you are a mouse in the church try to find something to eat?

My beautiful Guardian Angel, I am the man I am because of you, I would never defile our commitment because it was given from God, and God help me if I ever did, I realize you are a very busy young lady, and my prayers are with you, I always think about you, and I will always think about you you have left an indelible mark upon my mind only through the grace of God in the Holy Spirit that works through me making me aware of the love that is out there for me, and that is a miracle in a way that we came about only through the grace of God, as I have been to before God takes care of me very well one moment at a time, and

I am very blessed, and for that, I thank God and pray to God, letting him know how fortunate I am to have a guardian angel sent to me is beyond my comprehension. I pray for your happiness and joy, and I will never betray this love that I have for you. You will always be my Northern treasure and my beautiful Guardian Angel. Please bring a lot of joy to others, and keep in mind my prayers are still with you and your Mother as well,

I realize you and your Mother are going to Sicily and then to France and have a lot of work to do for both of you. Keep in mind that my prayers are with you both and my love especially for you and that there is an American boy from Arizona who thinks about you and praise for you that you will be protected through the grace of God, God blessed with love and prayers my love,

God takes care of me very well once again, and I am blessed for that. Unfortunately, at this time, God only provides for me one moment at a time, and if I have said anything to have offended you or make you sad, can you please forgive me? Because you are my girl

Thomas wrote;

My beautiful Guardian Angel of whom God has drawn us together to save many other souls, I feel we realize how much we care for one another through God's grace and the strength and the love we have for one another. You are right, and there is so much more of our love that will be revealed.

You are so precious, and I'm so in love with you. Once again, my homeless apologize for making you feel sad when I mentioned to you about other men in your life that could take care of you better than I could, for some reason. I'm trying to be honest with you, and you realize honesty and the truth are like peeling an onion. Some tears are shed every time we peel a layer.

Sometimes it is worse in others, and I will never put another man before our love through God's grace that has brought us together that would be defiling the passion that God has for us. I am just realizing this now as I am writing to you. For some stupid reason in my head, I figured that you might be able to find someone to take care of you better than I can at this time. And it hurts my feelings to say those words to you because that would break my heart if you find another man to tell you the truth.

I would cry like a baby, and I would never forget you because you are my girl, and I am in love with you. I'm going to send you my feelings right now before I lose this, a smile I am capable of, a double smile. You're my girl. I am in love with you. Peace and grace of the Lord be with you and your Mother. Please make sure your Mother knows how much she means to me in my life for having a daughter such as yourself, and your Mother gave birth to my guardian angel. Your Mother's intuition, without even knowing me, letting you know to respect me right from the start should have told me something, and sometimes I have to be hit on the head several times before I get it, quadruple smile with a big grin.

I call him a slimy non-God-loving civilian and a communist. That's how I referred to Brian. He forgets everything, loses everything, is very messy, and does not take care of himself. Unorganized, my Ford sport tract Explorer is in the shop right now getting repaired because of Brian.

And this is not funny. I felt like killing him. I did put the fear of God into him once again as I find myself doing from time to time, he knows what I say I mean what I mean I say, although he makes me laugh because he is so simpleminded like Noah was when he built the ark, God has a reason for simpleminded people. Anyway, sweetheart, I love you and miss you, and I'm going to pick this email up where I'm leaving off right now because I love you I'm in love with you God loves you, and God loves us, and you are so precious, and I am so proud of you I pray your day is going well and how are you feeling sweetheart? God blessed you with love and prayers from your Zoro.

29 December 2018

DiAnnie wrote;

Good afternoon to the best man in the world!

How are you doing today? I hope that you're going to have a great day. Mine started long ago, and I can say so far so good. Sorry that I was unable to message you last night. I got so tired after I got back home.

Whenever I see my beautiful Guardian Angel, believe me, it makes me smile so hard, and I say in my heart this man knows how to have his lady connected to him. I appreciate all your lovely compliments, and these make me feel so special. I hope you never change and that our love for one another will be endless like I always say. As long you can be honest and tell me how much I play an essential part in your life, I rest assured that you truly understand my heart. You're right. No matter how things have to be like, the fact is God takes us through day by day. I thank Him for my own life, that of my Mom and yours. He will continue to take us through day by day. He only wants us to acknowledge Him that He is our creator. So please never betray this love I have for you. As long you leave out a mistrust, doubtful about my love for you, I will always be there for you.

It's the only way we can go on a smooth path with each other because when a person makes his or her own heart insecure, it is when insecurity comes in the heart. Then that person becomes anti-social and is against anyone, sometimes people, it's the Devil, but through it's how we position our hearts to live daily, it will depend on how we will treat others. Ourself is Satan anyway, so sometimes people are right about that saying. Sure, honey, we have a lot ahead of us.

My Mom alone can handle traveling alone, and it's only through prayer that we can achieve those problematic tasks ahead. When you are in the Lord, there's nothing to fear, so I know all will be. Sicily and France are on the agenda, but we may also travel to other places, not sure yet, though. I know my Arizonan American boy is my strong prayer warrior. He has been in physical combat before, so he knows how to protect me against physical and spiritual opposition. You have been forgiven many times, and I think next time will not just be by words; I will surely knock on your stubborn head..lol.

You're so funny..lol I didn't say money isn't necessary; I only tried to tell you it isn't everything. Sure, you're right, there will surely be a big wrestling arena because a $100 bill to people is so important, and taking it away would mean you are accepting they're all, so whenever the fights start, blame yourself for the battle because you took their dollars. Lol. I am not sad or stress right now especially reading your messages. It makes me laugh, and I can't stop smiling as I write to you,

I love your sense of humor so much. If you don't want your treasure to be sad, don't put up a fight because the fight will only bring out tension, and then we both will start regretting why the fight started in the first place. You think you're poor, right? Try to resettle in poorer countries, and my Mom was telling me that when they went to the Republic of Benin, she felt like helping everyone there, when she and Uncle Samuel when there the other time, and then to Italy while those Roma people are they beg before eating, so when you say you're poor think honey again, people are living below less than a dollar a day but still happy for life, so if you are a church mouse go to one of these developing countries and join millions of other church mice I think you will get on the plane back to Arizona. Lol, you DiAnnie try it, boy? No worries, wherever I am, I will surely let you know, we will contact each day like we are now, and nothing will change. Okay? Don't worry. Just pray God can help us.

Good, you realize that my eyes are not on another man unless you decide not to love me again then. Usually, I will have to find someone, but nothing has changed, and my heart and soul focus on our love. God knows my heart, and as a lady, my body is supposed to be the temple of God. Right, I have had an ugly past, but since I decided to put my trust in God, I am not the same again, and I must not jump from man to man just because of financial reasons. We are not taking anything from this world, I didn't know before, but since I got saved, there's a lot of change in my life.

Sad for Brian at his age, many people like that, from their youth they didn't care less and then age, catch up with them. Very sad how people live their lives without paying attention to what their lives are turning into. You're the God sent in his life. If not, I believe he would have been on the streets. Please don't give up on him. So how are you getting around since your car is in the shop? It must be sad and frustrating. You are a good man, honey. If not with all that Brian does, you would've thrown him out ever since. Continue to help him and teach him God's ways. It is never too late for anyone.

Well, I understand, and I know not everyone knows how to manage funds. Some people are so bad at it, and I guess that may be one of your challenges. When we are together, I'll help with that. I will make sure some unnecessary spending will stop to have those most important things. I hope that you repair your car soon so that things are much easier for you.

I think they want to force you to agree with them. That's very sad how they try to treat you. Good, you have your basic needs, which is essential. Well, about your children not letting you help others, they are right in a way, they are the ones working for their hard earn.

So it is expected that they only want to help you with it, not with others they have no relationship, believe me not everyone that thinks Godly like you and I. Very difficult for people to be calm when it comes to money. You can not work anymore, so don't regret that. God knows it all. Hahaha, I knew it! I knew if you had a lot of money, your eyes would've been everywhere looking for ladies, good. You were honest about it. I like you for that. Lol.

Thanks very much for understanding me. When I don't write sooner, it's never intentional one thing I will like you always to remember. I like it when I am in touch with you forever. You see how much I put in the time to stay in touch with you even though a lot is going on in my life and sitting writing all these messages must tell you how much I am focused on you, you write much because there's a software.

Still, I have none and do write you from my fingers sitting and writing you all this, and it does not bother me writing you if I have to take a whole day writing you it does not bother me at all, what bothers me is when you say harsh things to me knowing much I put in the time to stay in touch with you. My Mom does not see you anymore as a stranger. We both see you as a family in our lives because it has been almost a year, so how would we see you as a stranger? The only thing that may make it seem we have not met yet, which I know is inevitable in 2019.

We will see how it is there and then to know what kind of person you. Honestly, I know you are a free and nice gentleman, but they say seeing is believing. For us, we love you and see you as our own. So no worry or stress, you are just the person for me.

Sure, since we met and up till now I also ask myself that you haven't changed at all, you still looks the same way when I met you. I think you have a special favor from God. He likes you and has you in this world as promised how we will be in Paradise.

I think you have told me about the history of the Song Amazing grace, it is fascinating, and it looks new each time in my ears. Lol, don't forget to be writing your part of the song we plan to record when I get there. I will give you the French mixed with English guess people will like it..lol You're a great singer to me. I remembered when you recorded your voice on my phone the other time singing..do you remember?

Wow, a lot went on during Christmas and the eve. I read it all, and it's exciting! Mine, unfortunately, didn't go as I plan. My friend from church in Laval, a bit drive from here, had me serving as a nurse in the hospital, so much didn't go on, only going to church.

Thanks for your lengthy messages, and I always enjoy reading them all. I will try to get a few things together and maybe go out later. Enjoy your day. Gros issues a toi!

30 December 2018

Thomas wrote;

You are my precious Guardian Angel; I have never heard of anyone communicating as long as we have online without meeting first. Have you? When you get ready to travel with your Mother, please know that my prayers are with you and your Mother. Have you ever travel with your Mother to the extent that you're going to travel to Sicily and France and any other places you should decide to go with your Mother? It must be exciting for you, looking forward to traveling with your Mother to so many places you have not been before and only heard about. I know when I traveled throughout Europe when I was in the Marines. I also, as your Mother, have seen a lot of poverty in foreign countries. I should say another thing we have in common is that we were both from the North American continent, out of seven continents.

Can I tickle you when I see you? A smile. I'm not sure if that would be a good impression on your Mother. I'm not sure if your Mother knows of my sense of humor and how I like to laugh and make people laugh. I pray to God she gets used to it because I will never change in that area or my sense of humor.

If I can take people's minds off their trials and tribulations for a small amount of time, it is worth it. To make people laugh and to have fun makes them feel younger and good about themselves.

Precious, you are precious and costly. How are your knees doing?

And how is the weather where you are at? Questions questions questions questions do you ever feel you are being pressured into an interrogation? Double smile with a big laugh. I'm only kidding tonight. Take me seriously. That's right, I said tonight, a smile you can take our love seriously when we are hugging and kissing. I know one thing for sure we will have fun together when we finally do get together.

Do you think your Mother and yourself will beat me like a redheaded stepchild? Double smile with a big grin. I realize you can tying me up and hitting me on the head to get my attention. Only God knows what your Mother is capable of doing to me, smile smile smile I think I'm smiling I may not be smiley when your Mother gets done with me, big grin.

You have a good day, sweetheart, and I will wait to hear from you again once again I do appreciate your long emails, and if you do not have the time, I understand. My prayers are always with you because God loves us and our love for one another. Make sure and let your Mother know that my prayers are with her as well, and I most certainly capable of taking care of you and your Mother to protect you from anyone that should choose to mistreat you or your Mother. God help them.

I love you. I'm in love with you. God bless with love and prayers. Have a good day, beautiful. You are my girl, and I'm in love with you. I will work out for as long as possible and then lay down for a little while and then get up and write a couple of miracle stories. I was the witness.

I cannot get my mind off of you, Mrs. How many grandchildren do you feel your Mother would like to have? Smile, and please keep in mind I'm not going anywhere until we both have witnessed the birth of our grandchildren. God has kept me good-looking and young for a perfect reason; please do not feel obligated to send me a long email only if the spirit moves you, and please, by any stretch of the imagination, do not think I am pressuring you. Those are not my intentions, okay?

My beautiful guardian angel was sent from God, who I appreciate without reservation. God has inspired me with the love that will be eternal. You are so precious in my eyes and the eyes of God. Our love will be witness to others. I am doing fine, beautiful, because you are my girl that I am in love with—and sending me these lengthy emails to make my heart sing that my girl is truly in love with me and to file that in any way, shape or form would make the grace of God an accomplice to evil and this I have no intentions. Our love is a unique and God-given gift through the grace of Jesus Christ, our Lord.

Have you ever thought of what you would do if you had $20 million? Think about it? I would be interested in hearing or reading what you would do with so much money of blessings and abundance from God. What would you do with it?

I have put some thought to this question, and the answer I came to was even after tithing, I would not want that responsibility of possibly ruining other people's lives of whom I would be thinking of helping, would only destroy their lives and send their souls to hell and mine as well.

Just something to think about, I love you, I am in love with you, and peace and grace of the Lord be with you and your Mother through Jesus Christ the Lord's name amen, I'm going to start another email. You are such a sweetheart. Sending me such a long email draws me so close to you because I know you are a very busy, beautiful young lady, and to have time for me, especially the time that you put into writing and sending me this long email, is so precious and miraculous makes my miraculous love for you so strong. I love you, DiAnnie

DiAnnie wrote;

Good morning my Zoro!

It's the last Sunday of the year, and we will be heading for a brand new year. This reminds me that God is indeed watching over us. How are you doing this day? I hope you have a good night and that today brings you joy.

You make me so happy with all your sweet words, you're a great guy, to admit, and I feel so connected to you for the fact that you know how to make a lady feel so secure and free in your world. That's one of the big secrets most men don't know about, you have such great qualities, but I believe the reason you have had a sad past with ladies is the simple fact that they didn't understand you or knew how to deal with you or say you were not met to be.

So God has been keeping you alive for this moment between us. God's plans are always different from ours, and He takes years sometimes to do a simple thing. Our kind of time or years is not precisely His, so even though we might sometimes be tired of waiting. It's like you're waiting for a minute for him and complaining that it has been a year already. Lol, I think we follow God and not understand Him because if we want to understand Him from a human point, we will only disbelieve Him.

I haven't forgotten about my birthday. That's the last thing to do, I would unless I had brain damage and lost my memories..lol it is still loading, and I'm counting the days.. lol one good reminder for my birthday is when I think about the day Thomass Dad was born then I don't think there's a reason to forget right? It would be a great deal to be spank when we meet. I like those rough plays, so spank me well because when it's my turn to tie you, it will be terrible for you ..lol, because you will get your freedom from the ropes in many hours..hahaha I'm a bad girl.

My Mom knows my rough plays and jokes with her. She gets furious sometimes, but mind you, she like pranking people too..lol so I think we will be three crazy people..lol She will like your sense of humor she's a fun person. Mom is doing great, and everyone is looking up to New year in a day. She said to greet you and wish you a Happy New year in advance.

We are doing great so far.

Ah, what I like doing that makes me happy? Yeah, you have shot me with many tough questions and not bad at all. I have many hobbies. I love music, reading, movies, traveling, hanging out with my partner or good friends, work is compulsory. Hence, not one of what I like doing, I wished this world was the promised Paradise that no one needs to work, but our world isn't that way, so I get busy working because I need to survive, pay bills and get my dynamic needs. Sure, when we meet you in Arizona and stay with you for a few weeks, I will know you and the kind of person you are. I am smart ..lol. I think we started communicating in February or March of this year, not sure because it would take me days checking all our emails. I think that's not so important. We better focus on the future..lol. Yes, I saw a few profiles and messaged a few, and I got responses from, I think, three, including you, but most turned out to be just beyond my liking. They were not friendly at all.

I think a guy from Nova Scotia was vulgar to me. He was a pastor, he said, but I don't believe he was a true man of God. I think I told you about him before, not sure you will remember still. You're right. I did message you first. I wasn't sure you were also a nice guy because your first messages were naughty, but we got along well more than all I met, and here we are today.

Oh yes, I asked you to take your profile off because that was the only way I felt you were severe and was a one-woman man. I did delete mine as well. Yes, we did chat on yahoo, which was more comfortable and private but no longer functioning. When I get a good phone, I'll look for a friendly app for chat and let you know, I don't mind chatting, but emails are also useful because you sit and put your thoughts out. I know you have more time than me, but writing from time to time isn't bad. Whenever I delay, know that it's never intentional.

I will always stay in touch. Good, you do understand me, and I like this attitude about you so much. Oh, that's cool that you work out. It is suitable for health. I see why you are fit and still looking young every time. I know your secret now..lol.

Yes, I remember you told me about growing up naturally. I think this paved the way that you are who you are today,

God has His plans for us each time, and your Dad he did well for you all.

The hard life you had made you more substantial, and today you're the very great Thomas that you are. You served your country that alone is greatness in a way. You're right. It is not a joke. Some people get called home not according to their will, some young people but starvation, which is very sad because they have very corrupt governments who do not care for their people. That's one of my plan and hope in this life, to help poor people,

If I had the $20 million that you asked me about, the charitable purpose would go to those people because I would travel to those places and see and meet the actual people and help them. That is what Christ instructs us as Christians to do, help the orphans *and widows. Whenever we put ourselves in other people's shoes, we realize that we are doing the will of Christ. It makes us not be limited to our localities. No worries, my Mom and I are indeed close and family. It's not impossible to have this good God-fearing Marine a part of us. Sure lack of father figures in many families make children live their own lives,*

I almost got stuck in that, but good, my Mom, was healthy and never gave up on me. I like your positive attitude, especially not mistreating women or men that do that. I saw that a guy in the US raped a three months old girl and is on the run. Why are some men so heartless! I pray that he is caught and tell why he was so blinded. I am glad that you will always protect us, It makes me cry because that's what my Dad did and always told me that he would give his life for us, but here we are today without him, make me think his spirit still grieve seeing us all alone, so having you mean a lot to us more than you know.

Well, it is only those who are interested in each other that would communicate so long without meeting first. When God is in someone's life, their understanding is quite different than those still believing in themselves. This is a great testimony that we will tell people on our wedding day. People would be so amazed and will realize that God is the only way out. I appreciate your prayers each time, my love, and please continue to do as we travel. I will keep you updated each time. As long we continue to stay in touch, you will know how things are going every time, so no worries.

Sure traveling will be exciting for me because I have always wanted to see places I have heard of, if not all just a few places, you have more experience than me because you travel many places because of your job. I wish I knew you then and was also in the Marine, but then I wouldn't be this young..lol You want to tickle me? We will see. I don't think my Mom would have any problem as long it isn't in a rude way. She will like your sense of humor. She is a fun person. So I don't think it's going to be a big deal. I have told her many times that you are a funny guy and make people laugh a lot. She will like you because not even meeting you. We have already selected you.

I am generous, and my knees are in good shape recently, so I am thankful because this holiday season if they acted silly, I would have been so disappointed. Thanks so much for your prayers. The weather is still cold here, but we are managing. Oh no, I'm not pressured at all about all the questions. Someone that cares would ask all these questions, I sometimes do, and you don't mind, so no, we are cool. I love the fun, honey, and I know our love will always be taken seriously. I know you're a silly guy, so I don't take you seriously at times because you are a fun guy. I enjoy your messages and make it as if we are right before each other.

One cannot be overconfident. Hahaha, my Mom would not handle those 12 kids and grandkids. You want two or three would be cool for her. I know you want more.

You're bad on Brian..lol I know you're just kidding. We will make Brian a better person before he is called home. I hope your vehicle is fixed soon. Well, my love, I'll send this off to you now. Hoping your day goes well. Mine is going well so far.

I love you so much and can't stop thinking about you as well—hugs and kisses from me.

Thomas wrote;

Beautiful, my guardian angel, you make me laugh. How on God's green earth do your knees act funny? Do you know what I have never had in my life that makes our love real? I have never had a lady that even mentions or loves God the way that you do. And that is what makes me love you more than you'll ever know because to the grace of God is the reason we are together, and your father and my father spiritually would like us to be together. Your father knows I will protect you and your Mother no matter what. And my father's birthday is on your birthday, and knowing my father, he would want a godly woman in my life. Because he believed in God and realized or understood how hard it is or difficult to find a lady who believes in God nowadays? You are very special. I'm not sure if I would ever tickle you in front of your Mother. That would be for the two of us lying in bed together with one another having fun.

I have learned through living a couple of years more than you have that when we get called home by God, it will be his time, not ours, no matter what.

I'm excited for you traveling and getting to see some of the worlds that you have never been to before. Because I know in this way, you will have a great appreciation for the freedom we. Live in. And yes, I did hear about that guy that rate that three-month-old girl. What does not come out in the wash will undoubtedly come out in the rinse. In other words, it may seem like some people do not get rightfully punished for the crime until they face Jesus Christ and the final judgment. You are so precious I could just pinch your cheeks, smile, and double smile. Yes, you did mention that minister that you had contact with, I'm not passing judgment on ministers, but I have found that many are not who they proclaim to be.

Because of their ego, I am easing God out. They will be judged very severely for the crimes they do amongst their parishioners. I'm so in love with you, and I think about you continuously. Maybe I did not make myself clear. You are so funny. You make me laugh, oh K, let us assume you had $40 million, no let S raise the bar, $143 million. I chose that amount because I know the lady in the Safeway grocery store who sold the guy one ticket for the lottery, and he won $143 million. I did not give you enough money to spend LOL I just gave you a raise from $20 million to $143 million. LOL, with a big smile and a double backflip with a big triple grin. Now, what are you going to do? My beautiful precious Northern treasure? I'm interested and hearing what you would do with that much money just for fun. I feel receiving that amount of money and being the minister that mistreats others or abuses them in my personal belief. There is no difference. What do you think?

Just change the subject now. I believe through the grace of God. We would only have 12 children if most of them were adopted, and we had the money and opportunity to take care of them. I would certainly not want you to have 12 children, of course, that would you be your decision, there is no greater joy in this whole life that God has given to parents as to raise those children properly like your Mother has done with you and provided you with morals and an intelligent with an intuition that the majority of mothers do not do for the daughter. And for that, I thank God for her graciously. As far as the emails go in the time we met, the farthest I can go back in our meeting was 15 February, this I have documentation of. I was just curious if you found anything sooner than that.

And from that email, I found 15 February. It appears to me as we met before that, and I cannot see exactly when. You are such a precious God-given gift. This is why I continuously think about us, primarily because God provided a way for us to meet. It was a miracle in my mind that we are still together after one year of communicating, and the only reason is we are equally yoked spiritually. This love I have never had before, and I thank God with my prayers daily for you and your Mother and myself that we had come together in the timing of God's will through the Holy Spirit and Jesus Christ the Lord's name this we pray for before we met.

The miracle in my mind is your intelligence and intuition that can foresee the love that will grow between the two of us. To help many others in their marriages but raise a family and help others and so many other ways. This is why I feel that God will inspire us with an overabundance. And this will be the most incredible new year spiritually, I think, and this I pray for, that we will finally meet. I know with expectation spiritually that it will be more miraculous than our imagination could even imagine. I feel in my heart that no matter what, we will never come apart.

So you're going to tie me up and leave me, LOL. This I will enjoy immensely and turn me centrally with love desires—big smile with the double grin and a triple backflip. My pubic hair is coming back very well, big smile, and my testicles are just about an average, more giant smile with the double grin and a quadruple backflip

And I have dreams continuously about the two of us together, and I do not mean to be disrespectful. I'm not sure how big I will get between you and me because of this love that God has given us that neither of us has experienced before. I feel it will be spectacular and magnificent with satisfaction continuously throughout the rest of our lives together. Okay, that's enough of that, see what you do to me? You start making me think spectacular sensual love thoughts of the two of us. LOL, and God does not have anything against love or makings babies together; otherwise, we would not be here, right? Subdue the earth and become plentiful, as it starts in Genesis. It is the nature and the morality of loving one another that makes it right in the eyes of God.

I think I told you about this at one point in time, that two Merry gentlemen to each other adopt their three-month-old baby girl, and the state of Arizona condone that. Sick, sick, sick, an abomination against God for sure I cannot even imagine that little girl being raised by two men without a mother.

Anyway, let us change the subject. Please let your Mother know how proud I am of her for raising a daughter such as yourself, and that if it was not for your upbringing through your Mother's guidance and wisdom, more than likely, I would not be with this girl right now and only through the grace of God. I not only think of you and your Mother daily and continuously, I believe God through prayer and let him know my love for him and his son Jesus Christ our Lord. You are so precious, and when we first met, I had to question God about my thoughts of what I wanted and the lady God chose us to be together for life and eternity. How are you feeling? What have you been doing? Are you happy? Here go the questions again, smile with a big grin. What is your favorite color? What is your favorite flower? What kind of candy do you like?

What kind of precious stone do you want? What is your favorite food to eat? Anyway, and of questions for one email, LOL smile smile smile I am so proud of you for being the intelligent young beautiful lady with knowledge and wisdom that you are and has the intuitive insight to know a God-given love immediately when she recognizes it. Even if this dumb Marine, a smile, had a hard time realizing that love. I'm in love with you, and I thank God for that.

There is only one thing I fear, and that is God. For that, I am a God-fearing man. There is nothing or nobody that can put fear into me except God. So when it comes to protecting you and your Mother, as I have mentioned before, God helps them. Because the Devil certainly isn't. There are so many things I want to say to you and so much love I have for you and your Mother. It is difficult for me to explain in words. I feel that love will come when we meet one another. There is only so much we can say on the right on parchment.

The real of and the feelings of love will come through the experience of love. The spiritual connection with one another is when the holy grace of God will come through our spirits and connect in a way that we could never imagine, and your Mother yourself and I have prayed for this love for us on one level or another.

I will send this off to you right now because I do not want to lose these words. You are my girl. You are my guardian angel and the most precious love I could not have ever known without the grace of God. I love you, and I can hardly wait to give you big hugs and soft, tender kisses.

CHAPTER 8

Coronavirus God's Wake-Up Call To The World

Thomas and DiAnnie have written this chapter with compassion prayerfully for the world.

The coronavirus is a wake-up call from God to the world. Nothing happens perchance, and everything happens for a reason. DiAnnie and Thomas pray to God they will be a rapture when Jesus Christ comes the second time and takes God's elect up into heaven instantly—and not left behind for the tribulation of seven years of pure hell on earth.

To either take the mark of the antichrist and lose our soul for eternity in the depths of hell. Or have our heads cut off and not take the mark as a second chance to get to heaven. The prophets are envious of this generation that they prophesy in the Bible. The world will never recover from the coronavirus. Other catastrophes are going to occur throughout this world for God to get everyone's attention, that the time as we know it is drawing to a close and prophecy will be fulfilled. ***God's warning.***

BIBLE== *Basic Instruction Before Leaving Earth.*

The world situation is deteriorating rapidly, and those that are blinded spiritually will know the final judgment. There is no fear of God, for the reason God has been taken out of the schools. It may be referred to as hot tub Christianity; if it feels good, do it. How sad, 1 million years from now, we will either be in one of two places, heaven or hell. And what we do will determine our eternal destiny. God's gift to us is life; what we do with this life is our gift to God. Roe versus Wade, making abortions illegal through planned parenthood. The blood of 60 million babies is crying out to God. 80% of the homes in the United States and the world are growing up without a father figure in the family. The children of these families are turning to drugs, prostitution, and gangs. These children find their love through prostitution, drugs, and gangs, and young girls are being sold into the sex slave industry. 70% of men in prison grew up without a father figure in the family. 50% of rapists grew up without a father figure in the family.

There is no high higher than the spiritual high that offers total freedom that Jesus Christ, our Lord, went to the cross and shed his precious blood for our wretched sins. God came here in the flesh as Jesus Christ and Jesus Christ left us with the Holy Spirit. That moves throughout the earth, answering our prayers and between us to help one another, we are in the age of the Holy Spirit. Jesus Christ, our Lord will come like a thief in the night we know not when, not even the angels in heaven, only God our father.

And you have to have faith in the situations that have occurred in your life, like miracles. And many are blinded spiritually and have no faith, and they are atheist, agnostic, secular humanist, and anti-Semitic. Keeping it simple, the year 2021, the year of our Lord Jesus Christ, undisputed. Hypocrites are among us and the multitudes of precious souls. They have no fear of God because they have never experienced life or have never been taught discipline. And in the Bible, Jesus Christ, the prophets, and disciples referred to the end days of being as Sodom and Gomorrah or in the days of Noah.

2 Peter 2: 5. *And spared not the old world, but saved Noah the eighth person, a preacher of righteousness, bringing in the flood upon the world of the ungodly.*

Romans 1: 17-32. For therein is the righteousness of God revealed from faith to faith; as it is written, thou shall live by faith. *[18] For the wrath of God is revealed from heaven against all ungodliness and unrighteousness of men, who hold the truth in unrighteousness. [19]Because that which may be known of God manifests in them; for God has shown it unto them. [20]The invisible things of him from the creation of the world are seen, being understood by the things that are made, even God's eternal power and Godhead so that they are without excuse. [21]Because that, when they knew God, they glorified him not as God, neither were thankful; but became vain in their imaginations, and their foolish hearts were darkened. [22]Professing themselves to be wise, they became fools.*

[23]And changed the glory of the young corruptible God into an image made like to corruptible man, birds, four-footed beasts, and creeping things. [24]Wherefore God also gave them up to uncleanliness through the lusts of their hearts, to dishonor their bodies between themselves. [25]Who changed the truth of God into a lie and worshiped and served the creature more than the creator, who is blessed forever. Amen. [26]For this cause, God gave them up unto vile affections; even their women did change the natural use into that which is against nature. [27]Likewise, the men, leaving the natural use of the woman, burned in their lust one toward another; men with men working that which is unseemly, and receiving in themselves that recompense of their error which was meet.

[28]. And even as they did not like to retain God in their knowledge, God gave them over to a reprobate mind to do those things which are not convenient. [29]But filled with all unrighteousness, fornication, wickedness, covetousness, maliciousness; full of envy, murder,

debate, deceit, malignity; whisperers. ³⁰*Backbiters, haters of God, the spiteful, proud, boasters, inventors of all evil things, disobedient to parents.* ³¹*Without understanding, covenant-breakers, without natural affection, impracticable, unmerciful.* ³²*Who knowing the judgment of God, that they which commit such things are worthy of death, not only do the same but have pleasure in them that do them.*

God has promised to supply all of our needs, not all of our greed. If you proceed to do good things in life, good things will happen. If you move forward doing evil things in life, bad things will happen. What does not come out in the wash will most certainly come out in the rinse. If you do not receive your just punishment here, you will most certainly be judged accordingly by Jesus Christ, our Lord. On every thought, every word, what you do, and what you fail to do. We must all realize two things: we are all going to die, and we are all going to stand before the judgment seat of Jesus Christ, our Lord. Very few, if any, people fear God or the eternal destination in hell. This journey is not that long, and knowing a 6-foot hole awaits you at the end, that would be depression.

The world will never recover from the coronavirus and things will never be normal only become worse. Gun is the answer through Jesus Christ our Lord's name and the Holy Spirit we can pray and ask for forgiveness. No resentments no regrets, we cannot turn the clock back. All we can do is move forward growing along spiritual lines trying to do the next right thing.

2 Timothy 3: 1-31. *This also knows that in the last days, perilous times shall come.* ²*For men shall be lovers of their selves, covetous, boasters, proud, blasphemers, disobedient to parents, unthankful, unholy.* ³*Without natural affection, truce-breakers, false accusers, incontinent, fierce, despise those who are good.* ⁴*Traders, he, high-minded, lovers of pleasures more than lovers of God.* ⁵*Having a form of godliness, but denying the power thereof; from such turn away.* ⁶*For of this sort are they which creep into houses, and lead silly captive women laden with sins, led away with divers lusts.* ⁷*Ever learning and never able to come to the knowledge of the truth. Now, as Jannes and Jambres (these two warlocks threw down their staffs and there's turned into snakes, Moses threw down his team and Moses snake devours their snakes) withstood Moses, so do these also resist the truth; men of corrupt minds, reprobate concerning the faith.* ⁹˙ *But they shall proceed no further, for their folly shall be manifest unto all men, as theirs also was.* ¹⁰*But thou hast fully known my doctrine, manner of life, purpose, faith, long-suffering, charity, patience.* ¹¹*Persecutions, afflictions, which came unto me at Antioch, at Iconium, at Lystra; what persecutions I endured; but out of them all the Lord delivered me.* ¹²**Yes, and all that will live godly in Christ Jesus shall suffer persecution.** ¹³**But evil men and seducers shall wax worse and worse, deceiving and being deceived.** ¹⁴**But continue without in the things which thou hast learn and hast been assured of, knowing of whom thou has learned them.** ¹⁵**From a child, thou hast known the holy Scriptures, which can make thee wise unto salvation through faith in Christ Jesus.** ¹⁶**All Scripture is given by God's inspiration and is profitable four doctrines, for reproof, for correction, for instruc**tion *in righteousness.* ¹⁷*That the man of God may be perfect, thoroughly furnished unto all good works.*

God warned Sodom when he sent two angels and told Abraham God would destroy Sodom and Gomorrah with fire and brimstone. The two angels went into lots household, and what happened was all the perverted people were pounding on lots door wanting Lot to send out the two strangers. Lot offered his two daughters that were virgins instead of the Angels. These evil perverted people wanted the strangers, and the Angels blinded everybody roundabout the house. And the Angels warned Lot, his daughters and wife not to look back. Lots wife looked back and turned into a pillar of salt.

Isaiah 1: 9. *Except the Lord of the host had left unto us a tiny remnant, we should have been as Sodom, and we should have been like unto Gomorrah.* [10]*Hear the word of the Lord, you rulers of Sodom; give ear unto the law of our Lord, you people of Gomorrah.* [11]*To what purpose is the multitude of your sacrifices unto me? Saith the Lord; I am full of burnt offerings of rams, in the fat of fed peace; and I delight not in the blood of Bullock's, or of lambs, or he-goats.* [12]*When you come to appear before me, who hath required this at your hand to tread my courts?* [13]*Bring no more vain oblations; incense is an abomination unto me; the new moons and sabbaths, the calling of assemblies, I cannot go away with; it is in equity, even this solemn meeting.* [14]*Your new moons and your appointed feasts my soul hath; they are a trouble unto me; I am weary of bearing them.* [15]**And when you spread forth your hands, I will hide mine eyes from you; yes, when you make many prayers, I will not hear; your hands are full of blood.** [16]**Wash you, make you clean; put away the evil of your doings from before my eyes; cease to do evil.** [17]**Learn to do well; seek judgment, relieve the oppressed, judge the fatherless, plead for the widow.** [18]**Come now, and let us reason together, saith the Lord; though your sins are as scarlet, they shall be as white as snow; though they are red like crimson, they shall be as wool.** [19]**If you be willing and obedient, you shall eat the good of the land.** [20]**But if you refuse and rebel, you shall be devoured with the sword, for the mouth of the Lord has spoken it.** [21]**How has the faithful city become a harlot! It was full of judgment; righteousness lodged in it, but now murderers.** [22]*Thy silver has become gross, thy wine mixed with water.* [23]*Thy princes are rebellious and companions of thieves; everyone loves gifts and follows with after rewards; they judge not the fatherless, nor do they cause of the widow come unto them.* [24]*Therefore saith the Lord, the Lord of hosts, the mighty one of Israel, I will ease me of mine adversaries, and avenge me of mine enemies.* [25]*And I will turn my hand upon thee, and purely purge away thy dross, and take away all thy 10; 26. And I will restore the judges as at first, and the counselors as that the beginning; afterward thou shalt be called, The city of righteousness, the faithful city.* [27]*Zion shall be redeemed with judgment and her converts with justice.* [28]*In the destruction of the transgressors and the sinners shall be together, and they that forsake the Lord shall be consumed.* [29]*For they shall be ashamed of the oaks what you have desired, and you shall be confounded for the gardens that you have chosen.* [30]*For you shall be as an oak whose leaf faded and as a garden that has no water.* [31]*And the strong shall be as total, and the maker of it as a spark and they shall both burn together, and none shall quench them.*

And to the Christians, Jesus said, do you remember lots wife? In one of the shortest verses in the Bible, Jesus said, do not look back. The world reminds us of all the lust and riches that we will be judged accordingly in this world. John 3; 16. And God so loved the world that he gave his only begotten Son that whosoever should believe in Jesus Christ our Lord should not perish but have everlasting life.

Every one of the signs is being fulfilled right now. Only when we receive Christ, our name will be written in the book of life as a sign of Jesus Christ, our Lord's second coming. Of no man knows not even the angels in heaven only God the father.

And all we have to do is repent of our sins. This is why Jesus Christ, our Lord, went to the cross for the repentance of our Richard sins. And iniquity is repenting but doing the same old thing repeatedly, and these will not be saved. The judgment of God, the love of God in the coming of Jesus Christ it is the end of the age. The devil dominates this age. There is a judgment day coming for those living outside the law of Jesus Christ and God the father.

Think about it, Sodom and Gomorrah were located at the Dead Sea. And before fire and brimstone, it was a very green lush area of land and sought after. Now Sodom and Gomorrah is located 1260 feet below sea level and is the lowest place on earth. The fire and brimstone decimated and sunk Sodom and Gomorrah, never to be inhabited again.

And, Abraham asked Lot where he wanted to go because their servants were not getting along, and they were getting too big, and the flocks were getting mixed up. So Abraham, Lots uncle, gave Lot a choice. And Lot as his wife and they wanted to go to Sodom and Gomorrah for it was a very wealthy rich place to live in the world at the time.

Jesus Christ, our Lord, referred to Sodom and Gomorrah as well as the time of Noah when the end times shall occur. Sodom and Gomorrah were filled with immoral love, the lust of homosexuality beyond the imagination very similar today. The first sin of Sodom and Gomorrah was their false security. They thought absolutely nothing to provide them with the world's insecurity and did not even recognize God. They were into their lustful greedy placers, and that was their second sin. Sin is remarkably joyful for a minute, and then it becomes depression and guilt. *The Scripture says there is pleasure in sin for a minute, not eternal, and our soul's journey. The brevity of life is but a twinkle of an eye as described as the shortest time in the Bible. Where are you going to be 1 million hours from now? Do you have a soul?*

Psalms 53: 1–6. To the chief musician, a Psalm of David. The fool has said in his heart, and there is no God. Corrupt are they and have done abomination iniquity; none does well. God looked down from heaven upon the children of men to see if they were any that did understand; they did seek God. All of them is gone back; they are all together become filthy; none does good, no, not one. Have the workers of iniquity no knowledge? Who eat up my people like the bread; they have not called upon God. There were they and greater fear, where no fear was; for God has scattered the bones of him that encamps against God; now has put them to shame, because God has despised them. Oh, that the salvation of Israel was coming out of Zion! When God brings back his people's captivity, Jacob shall rejoice, and Israel shall be glad.

The fool in his heart says no to God. He does not say there is no God; the fool says no to God. Then another Sodom and Gomorrah sin was overindulgence of sex, food, money, drinking, eating, homosexuality, and sexual pleasures with animals and treachery. The lowest level of hell frozen under ice alive, most evil is best feeling they cannot be described is eternally.

We would like to have Sodom and Gomorrah's fun employees without thinking that it is a sin to justify it, by our means, by possibly doing something good occasionally. We would like to have all that money, and sexual pleasure and that evil will come over us and what we will die in our souls lost for eternity. And we can die before our time at a moment's notice; before we confess our sins, our souls can be lost for eternity. The devil is very cunning powerful and baffling. The lust and greed of the world entices souls, is the only way the devil is able to get even with God to take as many souls to hell.

Luke 21: 1-38. *And he looked up and saw the rich man castor gifts into the treasury. And he'd also saw a certain poor widow casting in tethered to mites. And he said. Other truly I say unto you, that this poor widow has cast in more than they all. For all these have of their abundance cast in onto the offerings of God, but she of her penury. Cast in all the living that she had. He said some spoke of the temple, how it was adorned with goodly stones and gifts. As for these things which you behold, the days will come, in the which there shall not the left one stone upon another, that shall not be thrown down. (37 years later, Titus and the Roman army pulled the temple down) And they ask him, saying, Master, but when shall these things be? And what sign will there be when these things shall come to pass?*

And he said, Take heed that you be not deceived; for many shall come in my name, saying, I am Christ; in the time draws near; go you not therefore after them. But when you shall hear the words and commotions, be not terrified; for these things must first come to pass; but the end is not by and by. Then said unto them, Nation shall rise against Nation and kingdom against kingdom. And great earthquakes shall be in divers places, famines, pestilence, and fearful sights and great signs shall there be from heaven.

But before all these, they shall lay their hands on you and persecute you, delivering you up to the synagogues and into prisons, being brought before kings and rulers for my sake. And it shall turn to you for a testimony. Settle it, therefore in your hearts, not to meditate before what you shall answer, for I will give you a mouth and wisdom, which all your adversaries shall not be able to gainsay or resist. And you shall be betrayed both my parents, and brethren, and kinsfolk's, and friends; and some of you shall they cause to be put to death.

And you shall be hated of all men for my namesake. But there shall not a hair of your head perish. In your patient possesses you your souls. And when you shall see Jerusalem compassed with armies, then know that the desolation thereof is nigh. Then let them in Judea flee to the mountains, let them which are in the midst of it depart out, and let not them in the countries enter thereinto.

For these be the days of vengeance, that all things which are written may be fulfilled. But woe unto them that are with child, and to them that give suck, in those days! For there shall be great distress in the land, and wrath upon the people. And they shall fall by the edge of the sword, and to be led away captive and to all nations; and Jerusalem shall be trodden down of the Gentiles until the times of the Gentiles be fulfilled.

And there shall be signs in the sun, and the moon, and in the stars; and upon the earth distress of nations, with perplexity; the sea and the waves roaring. Men's hearts failing them for fear, and for looking after those things which are coming on the earth; for the powers of heaven shall be shaken. And then shall they see the Son of Man coming in a cloud with power and great glory. And when these things begin to come to pass, then look up, and lift your heads; for your redemption draws nigh.

And he spoke to them a parable; Behold the fig tree and all the trees. When they now shoot forth, you see and no of your selves that summer is now nigh at hand. So likewise you, when you see these things come to pass, no you that the kingdom of God it is nigh at hand. Verily I say into you, This generation shall not come to pass, till all be fulfilled. Heaven and earth shall pass away, but my words shall not pass away. And take heed to yourselves, (when Israel became a nation in 1948, the next generation shall not come to pass) less at any time your hearts be overcharged with surfeiting, and drunkenness, and cares of this life, and so that day come upon you unawares.

For as a snare shall it come upon all them that dwell on the face of the whole earth. What you, therefore, and pray always, that you may be accounted worthy to escape all these things that shall come to pass, and to stand before the Son of Man. And in the daytime, he was teaching in the temple; in the night, he went out and abode an amount called the Mount of olives. And all the people came early in the morning to him in the temple to hear him.

Jude 1: 11–25. *Woe unto them! For they have gone in the way of the Cain, and ran greedily after the error of Balaam for reward, and perished in the gainsaying of Core. These are spots in your feasts of charity, when they feast, with you, feeding themselves without fear; clouds they are without water, carried about of winds; trees whose fruit are without fruit, twice dead, plucked up by the roots. Raging waves of the sea, foaming out of their shame; wandering stars, to whom is reserved the blackness of darkness forever. And in it also, the seventh from Adam, prophesies of these, sayings,*

Behold, the Lord comes with 10,000 of his saints. To execute judgment upon all and conceive all that are ungodly among them of all the ungodly deeds they have ungodly committed and of all their hard speeches that ungodly sinners have spoken against him. These are murmurs, complainers, walking after their lusts; in their mouth speaks great swelling words, having men's persons in admiration because of advantage. But, beloved, remember the words which were spoken before the apostles of our Lord Jesus Christ. How that they told you they

should be markers in the last time, who should walk after their ungodly lusts. These are they who separate themselves, sensual, having not the spirit.

But you, beloved, building up yourselves on your most holy faith, praying in the Holy Ghost. Keep yourselves in the love of God, looking for the mercy of our Lord Jesus Christ unto eternal life. And some have compassion, making a difference. Another save with fear, pulling them out of the fire, hating even the garment spotted by the flesh. Now unto him, that can keep you from falling and present you faultless before the presence of his glory with exceeding joy. The only wise God our Savior, the glory and majesty, dominion and power, both now and ever. Amen.

No fear of God, 10 Commandments taken out of schools, the world wants to abolish the Bible, and Planned Parenthood authorizes abortions. Russia has troops station in Arabia. Persia or Iran will side with Russia, and the Islamic countries are all aimed at Israel. And Jerusalem is where Jesus Christ, our Lord, will ascend from heaven. And the dead in Christ will be caught up with God's elect and raptured. Then the antichrist is in the process of taking over right now and looking at the world situation and the deterioration of the world economy. If you take the mark of the beast on your forehead or your hand, you will lose your soul. You may have a second chance sting for the tribulation, seven years of pure hell on earth. As described in the book of Revelation. The Bible was inspired through the Holy Spirit, written by 40 authors of Jewish descendent, and it is understandable. Mathematics and prophecy cannot just be explained away.

Psalms 44: 1–26. To the achievements edition for the Son of Korah. We have heard with our ears, oh God, our fathers have told us, what work you did in their days, in the times of old. How did Drive out the heathen with thy hand, and planted them; although they did afflict the people, and cast them out. For they got not the land in possession by their sword, neither did they own arm save them; but thy right hand, and thine arm, in the light of the night countenance, because thou has a favor unto them. Thou art my king, O God; command deliverances for Jacob. We push down our enemies; through thy name will we tread them under that rise up against us. For I will not trust in my bow, neither shall my sword save me. But thou hast saved us from our enemies and has put them to shame that hated us. In God, we boast all day long and praise the name forever. Selah. But Dell has cast off, put us to shame, and goes not forth with our armies. Now make us turn back from the enemy, and they which hate us spoil for themselves. Thou hast has given us like sheep appointed for meat and hast scattered us among the heathen.

The house sells the type of people for not and does not increase the wealth by their price. Dow makes us a reproach to our neighbors, a scorn and the derision to them that around about us. That makes us a byword among the heathen, a shaking of the head among the people. My confusion is continually before me, and the shame of my face has covered me. For the voice of him that reproaches and blasphemy; because of the enemy and avenger. All this has come upon us; it has we not fought for you, neither have we dealt falsely in the night covenant. Our heart is not turned back, neither has a step's decline from the highway. Thou has sore brokenness in the place of dragons and covered us with the shadow of death. Suppose we have forgotten the name of our God or stretch out our hands to estrange God. Shall not God search this out? For he knows the secrets of the heart. Yes, for thy sake are we killed all day long; we are accounted as sheep for the slaughter. Awake, why sleeps thou, O Lord? Arise, Cass is not forever. Wherefore hides thou thy face and forgets our affliction and our oppression? For our soul, his bow down to the data; our belly cleaves unto the earth. Arise for our help, and redeem us for thy mercy's sake.

Luke 1: 1–32. Paul, a servant of Jesus Christ, called to be an apostle, separated unto the gospel of God, which he had promised before by heaven's profits in the holy Scriptures. Concerning his Son Jesus Christ our Lord, which is made of David's seed according to the flesh. And declared to be the Son of God with power, according to the spirit of holiness, by the resurrection from the dead.

By whom we have received grace and apostleship, for obedience to the faith among all nations, for his name. Among whom are you also the called of Jesus Christ. To all that be in Rome, beloved of God, called to be saints; Grace to you and peace from God our Father, and the Lord Jesus Christ. First, I think my God through Jesus Christ for you all, that your faith is spoken through the whole world. For God is my witness, whom I serve with my spirit in the gospel of his Son, that without ceasing, I make mention of you always in my prayers.

I am requesting if I might have a prosperous journey by the will of God to come unto you by any means now at length. For long to see you, that I may impart unto you some spiritual gift, to the end you may be established. That is that I may be comforted together with you by the mutual faith of both of you and me. Now I would not have you ignorant, brethren, that oftentimes I purposed to come unto you, but was let here too though, that I might have some fruit among you also, even as among other Gentiles. I am a debtor both to the Greeks and the barbarians, both to the wise and the unwise. So, as much as in me is, I am ready to preach the gospel to you at Rome.

For I am not ashamed of the gospel of Christ; for it is the power of God unto salvation to everyone that believes; to the Jew first, and also to the Greek. For therein is the righteousness of God revealed from the faith to faith, as it is written. They shall live by faith. ***For the wrath of God is revealed from heaven against all ungodliness and unrighteousness of men, who hold the truth in unrighteousness.***

Because that which may be known of God manifests in them; for God has shown it unto them. For the invisible things of him from the creation of the world are seen, being understood by the things made, even His eternal power and Godhead; for that, they are without excuse. Because that, when they knew God, they glorified him not as God, neither were thankful; but became vain in their imaginations, and the foolish heart was darkened. Professing themselves to be wise, they became fools. And changed the glory of the incorruptible God into an image made like a corruptible man, birds, four-footed beasts, and creeping things. Wherefore God also gave them up to the uncleanliness through their hearts' lusts to dishonor their bodies between themselves. Who changed the truth of God into a lie and worshiped and served the creature more than the creator, who is blessed forever, amen.

For this cause, God gave them up unto vile affections; for even their women did change the natural use into which it is against nature. (lesbians) And likewise, also men, (homosexuals) having a natural use of the woman, burned in their lust toward one another; men with men working that which is unseemly, and receiving in themselves that recompense of their error was meet. And even as they did not like to retain God in their knowledge, God gave them over two reprobate minds to do those things which are not convenient.

It is being fulfilled with all unrighteousness, fornication, wickedness, covetousness, maliciousness, full of envy, murder, debate, deceit, malignant eight, whisperers. Backbiters, haters of God, the spiteful, proud, boastful and boasters, inventors of evil things, disobedient to parents. Without understanding, covenant-breakers, without natural affection, and placeable, unmerciful. Who knowing the judgment of God, that they which commit such things are worthy of death, not only do the same but have pleasure in them that do them.

We worship our bodies, we adore our good times, and we spend more on cosmetics than we do worship God or Christ. Sodom and Gomorrah were most undoubtedly guilty of greed. God says that in Romans one that he gave them up three times. Has God given up on you? Have you given up on God?

Luke 14: 1–35.

And it came to pass, as he went into the house of one of the chief Pharisees to eat bread on the Sabbath day, that they watched him. And, behold, there was a certain man before him which had dropsy. And Jesus answered spake unto the lawyers and Pharisees, saying, it is lawful to heal on the Sabbath day? And they held their peace, and he took him, and healed him, and let him go. And answered them, saying, Which of you shall have an ass or an ox fall into a pit, I will not straightway pull him out on the Sabbath day?

And they could not answer him again to these things. And he put forth a parable to those which were bidden when he marked how they chose out the chief rooms; saying unto them. When thou art bidden of any man to a wedding, sit not down in the highest room; lest a more honorable man than now be bidden of him. And he that bade thee, and he comes and says to thee, Give this man place; and now begin with shame to take the lowest room. But when thou art bidden, go and sit in the lowest room; that he that bade thee, come, he may say unto thee, Friend, go up higher; then shalt thou have worship in the presence of them that's it at meet with thee.

For whomsoever exalted himself shall be a blessing; he that humble of himself shall be exalted. He also said he also wrote to them that bade him, When no makes a dinner or a supper, call not that I friends, nor thy brethren, neither the kings men, nor thy rich neighbors; lest they also bid again, and a recompense be made thee. But when now make a feast, call the poor, the maimed, the lame, the blind. And thou shalt be blessed; for they cannot recompense thee; for thou shalt be recompensed at the resurrection of the just. And when one of them that set at a meeting with him heard these things, he said unto him; Blessed is he that shall eat bread in the kingdom of God.

Then said he unto him, A certain man made a great supper, and bade many. And sent his servant at supper time to say to them that were bidden, Come; for all things are now ready. And they all, with one consent, began to make excuses. The first said unto him, I have bought a piece of ground, and I must needs Co. and see it; I prayed thee have me excused. And another said, I have bought five yokes of oxen, and I go to prove them; I prayed thee have the excuse. And another said, I have married a wife, and therefore I cannot come.

So that servant came and showed his Lord these things. Then the Master of the house, being angry, said to his servant, Go out quickly into the city's streets and lanes, and bring in hither the poor, and the maimed, and the Holt, and the blind. And the servant said, Lord, it is done as thou hast commanded, and yet there is room. And the Lord said unto the serpent, go out into the highways and hedges, and compel them to come in, that my house may be filled. For I say unto you, That none of those men which were bidden shall taste of my supper. And there went great multitudes with him, and he turned and said unto them.

If any man come to me and hate not his father, and mother, and wife, and children, and brethren, and sisters, yes, and his own life also, he cannot be my disciple. And whosoever does not bear his cross and come after me, cannot be my disciple. For which of you, intending to build a tower, sit not down first, and counted the cost, whether he have sufficient to finish it? Less happily, after he has laid the foundation and cannot finish it, and all that behold, it began to mock him. Saying, This man began to build, I was not able to finish. Or what king, going to make war against another king, sin is not down first, and consults whether he can with 10,000 to meet him that cometh against him with 20,000? Or else, while the other is yet a great way off, he sends an ambassador and desires it conditions of peace. So likewise, wherever he be of you that forsakes not all that he has, he cannot be my disciple. Salt is good, but if salt I have lost its savor, wherewith shall it be seasoned? It is neither fit for the land nor yet for the dunghill, but men cast out. He that has ears to hear let him hear.

CHAPTER 9

Thomas and DiAnnie

With all of our similarities through our faith our prayers and our love for God and the love we have never known. DiAnnie has changed Thomases life and continuously does so, Thomas with the Appreciation from this Guardian Angel treasure from the North country.

DiAnnie asked Thomas why he has remained single all of these years. Thomas had no answer, until DiAnnie and her mother Anna came into his life through prayer, faith and love for God and each other.

DiAnnie fatherless and her mother a widow, Thomas remains spotless for these years for a reason.

James 1: 27. Pure religion undefiled before God and the Father is this, To visit the fatherless and widows in their affliction, and to keep himself unspotted from the world.

We may never meet one another, over three years ago, we pray with faith and love for one another and God. And miraculously, through God's grace, we came together and have never parted. We are both ready for the rapture of Jesus Christ our Lord at any moment. Heaven is far beyond our comprehension or imagination, although God has a calling for us.

We keep God; first, we say our prayers together, devoting our lives to God and service helping others. We have found the love we could not even have dreamed.

We write this love of many manuscripts to be published, from another dimension that there is a love that miraculously God answers. Through our communication, we have developed this love beyond the theater of our minds; it's called « ***Agape.*** »

Together we pray, God willing, for a television series to help many hundreds of thousands of others, and if we only save one lost sheep, we have fulfilled our calling.

We have written through spiritual discernment, not-for-profit, or prestige, and our profits will be donated. And we thank God for contributors through prayer faith in God's love. And our mother, Anna, is a love, Thomas prays he can one day show her the love he would have liked to have shown his mother. Thomas loved his mother very much. And he misses her with tears from the heart, that one day we will be together again. And we thank God for another day together.

CHAPTER 10

Thomas poem to DiAnnie

You're free, you know, get some rest and let it go, and do not think of me, follow the path that God has laid for you and me. When we had taken God's hand and heard God's call. We came together to laugh, to love, to work, and to play. Accepted God's grace that brought us together this way. We found that piece at the close of each day. Our parting has not left a void for a reason, we remember the joy.

A friendship shared, laughing, and a kiss that we look forward to one day. Oh yes, these things we do miss. However, we are not burdened with a time we have spent together through God's holy grace and all the things we have in common that have brought us together one day. My friend, I wish you the sunshine of tomorrow that will show you happiness and no sorrow.

My life's been full and savored a dream of this love of my friend, and the good times one day will never draw to an end. A tear, a touch, our hearts that felt so much. Perhaps our time together seems so long, and we do not lengthen it now with our miraculous belief. We lift our spirits and peace for one another.

God wanted me to let you know, to set you free and let you go on with life's happiness and peace, until one day we finally meet.

The dream; I had three matches, one by one struck in the night, the first to see your face in its entirety. The second one I struck to see your eyes. The last match I struck was to see your tender, soft sweet lips. In the darkness was all around to remind me of all of these, as I held you in my arms.

God's love revealed through this romantic dimension of love

To be continued...

Printed in the United States
by Baker & Taylor Publisher Services